DECODING
YOUR GREATEST SUPERPOWER

ADAPTABILITY QUOTIENT

AQ

A NEW OPERATING SYSTEM FOR CHANGE IN AN EXPONENTIAL WORLD
THE SECRETS TO MASTERING YOUR BIGGER FUTURE

Foreword by BARRY O'REILLY
Author of UN LEARN and LEAN ENTERPRISE

ROSS THORNLEY

DECODING

YOUR GREATEST SUPERPOWER

ADAPTABILITY QUOTIENT

A NEW OPERATING SYSTEM FOR CHANGE IN AN EXPONENTIAL WORLD
THE SECRETS TO MASTERING YOUR BIGGER FUTURE

"Of all of the emotional intelligence competencies, strength in adaptability predicts success most often."

Daniel Goleman, Ph.D.
Author of the New York Times bestseller Emotional Intelligence and
Social Intelligence: The New Science of Human Relationships.

"DECODING AQ WILL EMPOWER YOU TO NOT ONLY BE ABLE TO ADAPT AND SURVIVE IN THE FUTURE WORLD, BUT TO THRIVE AND REALISE YOUR BEST SELF

—

EVERY DAY FEELING MORE CONFIDENT IN WHO YOU ARE AND WHAT YOU CAN ACHIEVE. "

ROSS THORNLEY

CONTENTS

FOREWORD

Over 2,000 years ago, the seed of a civilisation—a startup if you will—sprang into being on seven hills in central Europe. And that startup would go on to scale itself for over 500 years as one of the most remarkable economic and cultural powers the earth has ever seen.

At its prime, the Roman Empire occupied more than 2 million square miles and included approximately 20 percent of the world's population. And for centuries, scholars have mused what it was that brought Rome such tremendous success. Was it the empire's visionary leaders? Its armies? Its roads and aqueducts? Or simply its laws of governance?

In fact, it was none of these.

As philosopher Baron de Montesquieu explained, the unique innovation of the Roman Empire's success noted from when they engaged with other cultures, "they always gave up their own practices as soon as they found better ones".

And this unique ability to adapt, to unlearn what had brought it success in the past to succeed in the future, enabled this civilization to startup, scale, and sustain itself by letting go of the past to achieve extraordinary results—until this skill, to learn, unlearn, and relearn was in fact forgotten, triggering the collapse of Rome and a dive into the dark ages.

My inspiration to write *Unlearn: Let Go of Past Success to Achieve Extraordinary Results* came from what I frequently found to be a significant inhibitor when helping high-performance individuals get better—not the ability to learn new things but the inability to unlearn mindsets, behaviours, and methods that were once effective but now limit their success.

Ross has been struck by a similar insight, yet has gone well beyond instinct to scientifically understand, measure, and guide meaningful action to help people develop what is the key tenet of their future success: adaptability.

There comes a time in every individual's life when doing the things that brought you success in the past no longer delivers the same results. You wake up, and suddenly you're stuck, stagnating, unsatisfied, or struggling with what was once your secret to success.

The world evolves, conditions change, and new norms emerge. Instead of adapting, people find themselves stuck in their patterns of thinking and behaving. Most don't realise the new situational reality until it bites.

Those once-successful strategies can cause your downfall. The challenge is to make the adjustments and adapt.

I define unlearning as the process of letting go of, moving away from, and reframing once-useful mindsets and acquired behaviours that were effective in the past, but now limit our success. It's not forgetting or discarding knowledge or experience; it's the conscious act of letting go of outdated information and actively gathering and taking in new information to inform effective decision-making and action.

Ross defines adaptability as "the capacity to adjust one's thoughts and behaviours in order to effectively respond to uncertainty, new information, or changed circumstances."

Our missions are shared for what we want to bring to the world and the people that will shape it. Be reminded that good leaders know they need to continuously learn.

But great leaders know when to unlearn the past and how to adapt to succeed in the future.

Barry O'Reilly - Author international bestsellers, **Unlearn**: *Let Go of Past Success to Achieve Extraordinary Results*, and **Lean Enterprise**: *How High-Performance Organisations Innovate at Scale*—part of the Eric Ries series

AUTHOR'S NOTE

This book was originally conceived and drafted in 2018. However, in my heart, each time I revisited the final chapters, I did not feel happy enough to release it. When I returned to the book in 2022, I decided to take decisive and bold action and scratch the entire draft and start again. As painful as it was, I knew I had to live the very principles I was exploring and describing. This was an example of unlearning in action! I wanted to write a better book, so I had to let go of what went before.

The early draft of the book was not wasted, of course. Bits of it were salvageable, and it helped organise my thoughts and get me to where I am now. But ultimately, much of it— which didn't serve—had to be scrapped.

ON OUR JOURNEY, ONE OF THE HARDEST THINGS WE CAN DO IS LET GO OF WHAT WENT BEFORE OR WHAT WE THINK "GOT US HERE". HOWEVER, ONLY BY LETTING GO OF THE PAST CAN WE SEIZE THE BRIGHT FUTURE AHEAD.

INTRODUCTION

A s a species, we are currently navigating the most intense period of change that has ever existed in human history.

LET THAT SINK IN!

At no point in our 200,000 years on planet Earth have we ever had to cope with more rapid change. This is not to marginalise the significant suffering and challenges that we have faced and overcome (surviving the Black Death comes to mind); however, at no prior point have we ever been faced with exponential disruption on the scale that we see today. To quote an old maxim, "The way out is through." We can't run away from change. Instead, we have to learn to embrace and navigate it.

Decoding AQ is your playbook for unlocking your highest potential with the superpower of adaptability. Though this is a book about adaptability, **measuring the abilities, characteristics, and environmental factors which impact the successful behaviours and actions of people and organisations to effectively respond to uncertainty, new information, or changed circumstances**, it's also a book about fear: how it can control us, how it can shape our lives for the worse, but also how it can be used constructively. After all, our primate ancestors were probably wise to fear the lion, the crocodile, and the venomous snake. Fear can drive us, and sometimes letting fear "take the wheel" is the best solution. Fear will drive hell-for-leather if there's something scary to move away from, and there's plenty to be concerned about in the modern world: technological disruption, job loss, the widening gap between rich and poor, to say nothing of Four Horsemen of War, Famine, Pestilence, and Death who seem to be rearing their heads with gusto in our present decade.

Having said all of this—and perhaps painted a slightly bleaker picture than intended—there is one important thing to bear in mind that this book will reiterate time and again: as a species, we are cognitively biased to give more weight to the negative. Therefore, we must willfully, forcefully, and determinedly give light and attention to the positives. We must rewire our brains to escape the destructive cycles that keep many of us trapped in the biological past, unable to embrace our future. Yes, there is War, but there is also hope, kindness, deep acts of humanity, and collaboration. Yes, there is Famine, but we have more tools to tackle Famine than ever before. Welcome to our world of paradox.

I want to help guide you to uncover, expand, and release this immense potential and let go of the old ways of doing things which are no longer fit for purpose. But this is more difficult than it seems. Our brains are experts at holding onto information, reinforcing neural pathways, and protecting data. The idea of doing something differently, when what we did in the past worked, is a complete anathema to our genetic makeup. The idea of doing something without knowing the outcome—aka experimenting—is even more bizarre! Yes, we might have embraced this in our first years of life, and we have always had explorative scientists and maverick artists who went against this trend, but increasingly every single one of us is going to need to get much more comfortable with pushing the boat out.

My sincere hope is that *Decoding AQ* will empower you to not only be able to adapt and survive in the future world, but to thrive and realise your best Self—every day feeling more confident in who you are and what you can do. In the words of Leonardo Da Vinci, "One can have no smaller or greater mastery than mastery of oneself."

Over the course of this book, I'll be sharing many models and exercises in order to help you harness your adaptability intelligence. The intention is not that you complete every single exercise or utilise every single model (in fact, doing so might prove a bit of a headache), but rather to provide you with a range to choose from. Some of these models may be highly relevant, immediately applicable to your current business or situation, and some less so. There is no one answer to improving adaptability. The wood has many roads through it to the other side. We hope to provide you with as many options as possible so you can find the road that best works for you.

The first model I would like to share right at the outset of this book are the eight insights of an adaptive mind. In the mind-map below there are eight bubbles, each with an insight into a highly adaptable mindset. Let's unpack these a little bit:

1. FEAR TO FACT

We'll be covering this in the next section of the book in extensive detail, but the central take away is not letting your fear response, your amygdala, hijack your decision making ability.

2. LEARNABLE

Adaptability is improvable. It is not a psychometric trait, fixed and immutable. Think of adaptability like a muscle. With training, it can be strengthened. Highly adaptable people not only train their adaptability muscles but confidently believe in their ability to learn, grow, and improve their adaptability intelligence. For more insights into this principle, see the chapter on AQ-Ability in section 2.

3. LET GO

A principle we'll return to many times throughout this book is Unlearning: letting go of the past, of old methodologies that no longer serve us, in order to make room for the new. Letting go has always been an important principle in the spiritual and emotional sense, but in today's exponential world we're seeing just how vital it is in the practical sense as well. Businesses that fail to let go of arcane or outdated processes will struggle to survive.

4. PEACE IN PARADOX

The world is a very paradoxical place, where seemingly opposing truths can be simultaneously upheld. To unlock our adaptability we have to become more comfortable with paradox, remaining in ambiguity, and unafraid of uncertainty.

5. ENVIRONMENT

Our environment has a significant influence on our behaviours and our adaptability. We ignore it at our peril! Throughout this book we will explore ideas and techniques for curating your environment with intention in order to not only harness your own adaptability, but create a nurturing environment for those around you.

6.CYCLE

Our existence is made up of cycles: the seasons, birth-life-death, and the procession of the stars! The same is true of adaptability. In this book we will learn about the adaptability lifecycle and how to harness it in order to remain one step ahead.

7. THINK LONG — PLAN SHORT

Long term goals are of course important, but often we can "over plan" our steps toward them, and when life throws a curveball, we struggle to pivot. This is why we advocate to think long, but plan for the short term, using rapid feedback loops in order to collect data and test new approaches.

8. RE-MODEL

Shifting from reacting to response is one of the core principles of adaptability. When we "react" it is automatic and unconsidered (driven by fear, which links back to our first adaptive insight), but when we respond, it is measured, considered, and appropriate to the context. We'll be looking at this in more detail in part 4.

CONSIDER HOW THESE EIGHT PRINCIPLES MIGHT GUIDE YOU. EACH ONE WILL BE COVERED AT VARIOUS POINTS THROUGHOUT THIS BOOK. THE FIRST, FEAR TO FACT, IS THE FOCUS OF THE NEXT CHAPTER.

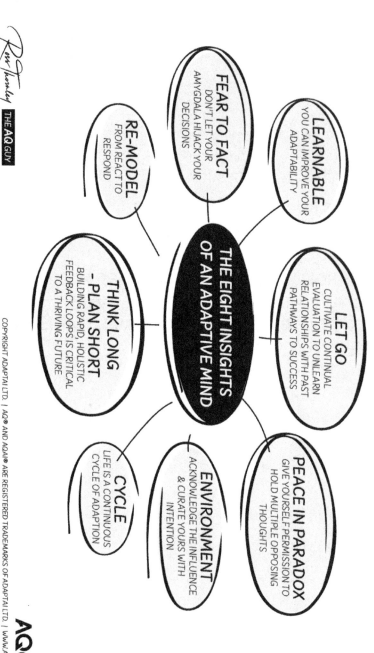

PART 1: FEAR TO FACT

THE FUTURE BELONGS TO THOSE WHO TRAIN THEIR ADAPTABILITY MUSCLE

There's a moment when the fear takes over.

It happens to all of us, though for very different reasons. Perhaps you've just received the results of a medical scan, or you're driving to a job interview—or firing up the Zoom call—with a company you've always dreamed of working at, or you've just jumped out of an aeroplane at fourteen-thousand feet. Maybe your company has just nosedived into bankruptcy with no signs of revival. Or maybe someone you've loved for decades has just told you they want to end it, and they love someone else. There's no way to sugar-coat these moments. They come like a thief in the night—to borrow a biblical phrase—and like a thief, the fear sneaks through our defences.

Although *homosapiens* have been around for approximately two hundred thousand years, when we are in the grip of terror, we act no differently from our primate ancestors, the mighty terrestrial apes. We fight, we run, we freeze. We seek safety in numbers. We beat our chests and show our teeth—frequently to no avail.

Our species has adapted to its circumstances and environment more than any other on the planet, and yet biologically we have changed very little. This has created a problem—and a paradox of sorts—for the human race in our current epoch of exponential growth and change: **WE HAVE MORE POTENTIAL**

THAN AT ANY POINT IN HISTORY, YET WE'RE SIMPLY NOT EQUIPPED TO DEAL WITH IT!

The importance of adaptability is so evident and so widely acknowledged—especially in the recent context of the Covid-19 pandemic and how it has altered everyday life, perhaps forever—it almost seems pointless to emphasise its significance here. However, it's clear that despite our longstanding relationship with adaptability, most of us are still struggling to adapt. "According to the Strategic Management Research Centre…" M. J. Ryan writes. "…the failure rate of mergers and acquisitions is as much as 60 to 70 percent. Why? Not because it's not a good idea to bring two organisations together to create efficiencies and synergies, but because the people in them fail to adapt to changed circumstances."[1] Suffice to say, the need for adaptability in our lives to cope with the rate of change has become more pertinent than ever, whether we are adapting to changes in our jobs or work routines, upheavals in our industry, new technology disruption, or even new global norms.

But what is adaptability?

Bruce Lee once said, "You must be shapeless, formless, like water. When you pour water into a cup, it becomes the cup. When you pour water into a bottle, it becomes the bottle. When you pour water into a teapot, it becomes the teapot. Water can drip, and it can crash. Become like water, my friend."

George Bernard Shaw observed, "**Those who cannot change their minds cannot change anything.**"

And finally, from H. G. Wells' Time Machine, "It is a law of nature we overlook, that intellectual versatility is the compensation for change, danger, and trouble. An animal perfectly in harmony with its environment is a perfect mechanism. Nature never appeals to intelligence until habit and instinct are useless. There is no intelligence where there is no change and no need for change. Only those animals partake of intelligence that has a huge variety of needs and dangers."

Change is the eternal constant and driving force of life and existence. Without it, what we really have is nothingness. Human beings are somewhat hardwired to fear change, but in truth, without it, we would not be where we are. In fact, human beings themselves might well not exist.

I also want to dwell on the statement: "an animal perfectly in harmony with its environment is a perfect mechanism." Human beings have always had a unique relationship with their environment. To be blunt, we have used and abused it like there's no tomorrow. Unlike many other mammals who establish an equilibrium with their environment, we tend to mine it for resources without adequate replenishment. I'm aware that I'm beginning to sound a little bit like a character from the original Matrix movie, but there's a significant degree of truth in the observation, and science fiction (as in the quote by H. G. Wells) has always been an imaginative expression of very real human concerns, hopes, dreams, and technological vision.

Not only is the human relationship with the environment problematic, we have also introduced a rogue element into our environment that is now adapting even *more rapidly* than us.

Technology.

Like Frankenstein's artificial man, we have created something which we are now uncertain how to control. And like Dr Frankenstein, we are soon going to face an important choice about how we treat our offspring. Do we reject it and blame it for all the world's problems? Or do we accept responsibility for our creation and learn how to work with it to create a better world? Can we change how we view technology and how we integrate it with our lives?

The Covid-19 pandemic has emphasised—more than ever—that many of us find the idea of uncertainty problematic, and can anyone really blame them? Human beings have a very uncomfortable relationship with the unknown. The cosmic horror writer H.P. Lovecraft profoundly observed, "The oldest and strongest emotion of mankind is fear, and the oldest and strongest kind of fear is fear of the unknown." For the majority of us, if we do not "know" what the outcome of an action will be, we tend to avoid doing the action! In an era that has been called "post-truth", where misinformation comes from every corner, including governmental bodies, **WE ARE IRONICALLY IN A PLACE AS A SPECIES WHERE WE KNOW MORE THAN WE HAVE EVER KNOWN, BUT WE ALSO ARE LESS SURE OF WHAT WE KNOW THAN EVER BEFORE.**

When we are afraid, when we perceive our environment as "antagonistic" or threatening, and when we are confronted with the unknown, our amygdala takes over.

The amygdala is the "reptilian" part of our brains, the stem that is directly plugged into the spinal column. The reptilian brain only really cares about survival. In terms of Maslow's Hierarchy of Needs, which despite being over 50 years old and considered outdated by some has continued to resonate with people, it sits at the very base of the pyramid, representing the lowest, most primordial urges. It governs breathing, our basic needs for food, sex, hydration, sleep, and the "fight or flight" response. In the past, of course, this part of our brain was extremely useful. With exposure to environmental stress stimuli, there is an increase in the release of amygdala neurotransmitters including glutamate, GABA, noradrenaline, and serotonin. Our amygdala goes to work in alerting the nervous system, which sets the body's fear response into motion with stress hormones like cortisol and adrenaline, in order to either fight off whatever was attacking us or run away at full speed. However, in the modern world, where the dangers that beset us are of a more intellectual, emotional, and societal nature, it often proves a hindrance. When we have been "hijacked" by our amygdala, our intelligent brain shuts down, and we can only compute two possibilities. Usually, both are quite useless. We cannot literally fight climate change. We cannot fight redundancy. We cannot fight a difficult exam. We can't run away from any of these things, either, except of course metaphorically speaking into the bottom of a bottle, drugs, or other age-old human ingenuities for attempting to dissolve our pain and trauma.

In the modern world, where the rate of change—and therefore the constant threat of the unknown—is increasing exponentially, we are continually being sent into fight-or-flight responses. Our amygdala is continually hijacking our thought processes and decision-making ability, and unless we can learn to overcome and reduce this outdated biological playbook, then we will not survive the coming change.

So how do we adapt?

The good news is that adaptability is not a Holy Grail that you need to go out and find. It is not something that can be pursued. It is already within you. Human beings have always had it. *You* have always had it. The difference is that now our environment has changed, and so some of the biological wiring and learning that once served our species is no longer helpful. In other words, none of this is your fault!

The natural human response to the unknown is either to flee it or to reach after certainty. Usually, the latter of these involves returning to something that is familiar. As the poet, John Dryden observed, "We first make our habits, then our habits make us." Habits can, of course, be a useful and powerful tool, but they can also become a negative cycle. You may have heard the phrase "un-learning" in recent times, and unlearning old habits and narratives is certainly part of the process that we will come to in time, but for now, let's focus on the basics.

Adaptability is not a personality trait, a Hippocratic humour, a corporate check-box, or the sole province of the highly imaginative or wealthy. Adaptability is a muscle, and like any other muscle, it can be improved over time and even more so with deliberate action. This muscle has been with us since the beginning, a superpower more potent than opposable thumbs or perhaps even our supercomputer-like neocortex.

The time has come for us to unlock this superpower and thrive.

EXERCISE 1:

You have had an introduction to some of the theory and history of adaptability, and its relevance to the modern world, but now it's time to get practical!

WRITE DOWN, IN JUST ONE OR TWO SENTENCES, YOUR DEFINITION OF ADAPTABILITY.

....

....

....

....

....

....

....

> Don't worry about "official" definitions; write about what adaptability means to you. As you explore adaptability throughout this book, you can return to your original definition and adapt it accordingly. This will not only give you a personal connection with adaptability but also show adaptability in action!

WHAT GOT YOU HERE WON'T GET YOU THERE

What Got You Here Won't Get You There is the title of Marshall Goldsmith's seminal book on the power of unlearning, published in 2008. This book is a challenging read because it asks us to question ourselves at the deepest level. As human beings, we tend to be very attached to "what got us here", and recognising that "what got us here" can only get us so far is a very painful lesson indeed. But let's look at an example of this in action.

In 1965, Gordon Moore published a paper observing the number of transistors on a circuit board was doubling roughly every twelve to eighteen months. This exponential progress of continual doubling was termed Moore's Law, and for the last fifty years has been observable in almost all of the technological progress we've made, from solar energy to computational power, 3D printing, sensors, AI, and robotics. The unstoppable momentum of technological advancement is evident in every microcosm of our everyday existence. As the 'S' curve of one technological improvement nests and converges with another 'S' curve, we see a continual uplift in accelerated growth. But this exponential change is not limited to the field of technology. A common misconception is that technology is an isolated province, of interest only to coders, technicians, and geeks. What innovators and thought-leaders like Peter Diamandis—author of *Abundance: The Future Is Better Than You Think* and founder of the X-Prize—

have shown, however, is that technology has a profound knock-on effect on our culture and way of life. Indeed, technology has caused the structures of our governments, organisations, and communities to shift dramatically. Consider the simple reality of widespread, interconnected "working from home" during the pandemic, a concept that would have been difficult to conceive of beyond small pockets of society merely a few decades ago.

In my first book, *Moonshot Innovation*, I described this accelerating exponential world we currently inhabit, where we're rapidly approaching and even living in a lightspeed pace of change.

New information is emerging every second. New studies are appearing on a daily basis unveiling fresh scientific and behavioural models. New technology is driving innovation in ways hitherto unimaginable. Consider how AI art has already transformed the possibilities of marketing, publishing, and other industries we haven't even considered yet. However, it's also likely that it could become redundant in an equally brief period, especially if organisations like MidJourney and DALL-E are forced to pay for the copyright of the classical art they import to create new images.

In times past, three years might have been an acceptable timeframe to bring an idea to market, but now, it is certainly too slow. The world is changing faster and faster, and we need to change with it. Companies that cannot diversify their offerings, change their business models, and radically pivot when new findings or legislation invalidates their previous processes or products will face sudden and dramatic extinction.

The challenge is that human brains are not wired for an exponential reality, they're wired for a linear one. We may *think* that we're all on board with change, but when we see the explosive speed with which a new piece of technology or a new methodology undermines our previous modus operandi and leaves existing paradigms in chaos, many recoil in disbelief, much in the same way that we might *think* that all life is sacred, but still flinch when a spider lands on our arm. The fear response is hardwired into us and unlearning it takes great patience, practice, and self-compassion.

The concept of cognitive bias was first introduced by Amos Tversky and Daniel Kahneman in 1972[2]. There are many forms of cognitive bias but the one that interests us most in this context is "embodied cognition", which is the tendency in human beings for selective perception, attention, decision-making, and motivation based on our biological makeup.

The brain has a tendency to hold on to negative memories or feelings. There's nothing "wrong" with this. It's a survival mechanism. If we turn west at a cross-roads and find ourselves at a lion's den, we are not likely to repeat the mistake if we remember the unfortunate event in vivid detail! This is why our successes and euphoric moments of triumph seem more transient and fleeting than our moments of despair. This is the tinted lens through which we view reality, our bias. Our brain is programmed to prioritise and focus on the negative, and it is programmed to "look back" for solutions to our current problems.

In 2008, Marshall Goldsmith published *What Got You Here Won't Get You There*. The narratives, methodologies, and strategies we used in the past are often no longer helpful to us. This is evident in behavioural psychology, where we observe the patterns we learned as a child that often trip us up in adult life. For example, if, whenever our parents shouted at us, we fled to our room and started comfort eating snacks, might it not be the case that in adult life whenever great pressure is exerted on us by a boss, a co-worker, even a lover or friend, we resort to the same thing? This is not to say that comfort eating is "wrong", per se, but in the above example, it is a learned defence/coping mechanism. Our unconscious paradigms have great power. Our worldview is composed of hundreds of these deeply ingrained narratives that we can hardly see but which inform our decision-making on a day-to-day basis. The reality is nearly everyone is dimly aware of this, as mental health is becoming a more widespread topic of conversation. However, most businesses and organisations do not realise that they also have company-wide narratives and paradigms informed by the collective mindset of their organisational leaders and people. Businesses make decisions based on past performances. They assess the value of propositions based on previous outcomes. It is the same survival process of avoiding the lion's den but playing out on a corporate stage, and a much larger scale.

This isn't to say our past is all bad, of course, but we have to recognise when we can use it, and when it reinforces a negative loop. If our environment has radically altered, and in an exponential world that is almost guaranteed to be the case, then is it likely that the same thinking will produce the newly required results?

Not very.

EXERCISE 2:

WRITE DOWN ONE ANXIETY OR CONCERN YOU HAVE ABOUT THE EXPONENTIAL FUTURE.

....

....

....

....

....

....

This could be a technological disruption, a change to work culture, or a more immediate threat. Try not to make it overly complicated

---

or overthink the exercise. Just consider something that impacts you right now or in the near future in your work.

NOW WRITE DOWN ONE OPPORTUNITY OR 'POSITIVE' THAT MIGHT COME OUT OF THIS CHANGE.

....

....

....

....

....

....

Try to be as specific as possible with both examples.

THE AMYGDALA HIJACK

What are the outcomes of these negative cycles? A simple answer would be "we die". This is because "cortisol and adrenaline are actually neurotoxic; that is, too much of them and they can harm or even kill off brain neurons."[3] Stress literally "shrinks" our brains.

In their study, "Resilience Training That Can Change the Brain" (2018), Golnaz Tabibnia and Dan Radecki stated that: "One of the challenges of consulting and coaching psychology is helping individuals, teams, and entire enterprises weather life and work stressors. These stressors can be one-time and acute, such as unexpected job transfer or job loss, or more chronic, such as bad bosses, broken peer relationships, and dysfunctional team members. Some people are more resilient than others in the face of such stressors, but many of the skills that make for resilience can be learned."

In other words, without Resilience, these "stressors", whether acute or chronic, can overwhelm us. We'll be diving into Resilience and how we can cultivate it at a later point in the book, but for now, I want to focus on the downstream impacts of stress and burnout.

The negative effects of stress and burnout on the individual are well understood by this point. When the amygdala has hijacked us, and we can only compute "fight or flight", our decision-making becomes significantly impaired. To make things worse, our brains are largely unable to differentiate between a life-threatening situation and one which is simply uncertain, unexpected, or unfamiliar. The brain offers the same response whether we are faced with talking in front of an audience of thousands or with a dangerous animal in the wild. This wouldn't be so much of a problem if we were easily able to dissipate this stress or fear response, but in the modern world, we cannot act on the fight or flight impulse in most situations. Therefore, we find ourselves in states of stress for *extended periods of time*. This means our decision-making ability is impaired not just in one particularly stressful instance but *long term*. Hence, our careers, our mental and physical health, and our relationships are all impacted. You will likely recognise some of the effects of perpetual uncertainty and anxiety when the hormones and neurotransmitters of Epinephrine and Norepinephrine, which are responsible for the adrenaline which is pumped through your body, are released: your lungs become more efficient and experience an increase in energy as sugar is released into the bloodstream from cortisol. Living in this sustained and prolonged state of physical stress negatively affects every area of your mental and physical health, from poor sleep to mood swings, heightened emotional reactions, low creativity and impaired ability to problem-solve.

As organisational leaders, there are even deeper consequences for succumbing to amygdala hijack and failing to adapt than simply those of personal burnout or failure—distressing and profound as these moments can be. We can literally drive our companies into the ground, thereby impacting all our employees, partners, and clients.

In the 1980s and '90s, MicroPro created a game-changing word-processing software product called WordStar. Widely respected technology expert John C. Dvorak heralded the software as "one of the greatest single software efforts in the history of computing." Due to the popularity of WordStar, MicroPro rebranded itself as WordStar International.

A simple name rebrand from MicroPro to WordStar may seem inconsequential in the grand scheme of business decisions. But the power of branding is not to be underestimated. The name shift was a mistake, a decision born out of a lack of confidence in the future that tied the company's identity to a single product. As advertising copywriter John Kuraoke explains, "As WordStar International, the company was poorly positioned to keep up with changes in the computer industry - such as the rise of integrated software bundles that were the predecessors to today's Microsoft Office. Note that Microsoft never became 'Windows International'."[4] In desperately attempting to capitalise on past success rather than look forward to the future, WordStar International fell into a trap of self-limitation. Between 1988 and 1993 the company struggled on, trying to sell variations of the original product, but the rise of competitors—including Microsoft Word—eventually led to their rapid decline.

EXERCISE 3:

WRITE DOWN ONE STRESSOR IN YOUR LIFE

....

....

....

....

....

....

(when you think of this, notice your heart rate increase, and perhaps your muscles feel like they tense up too). This should be something that stresses you but that is not overwhelming. We want to train our ability to deal with stress, so the trick is to start small.

NOW, WRITE DOWN WHAT THE LONG-TERM IMPACTS OF THIS STRESS HAVE BEEN.

....

....

....

....

....

....

Try to consider the impact on as many different facets of your life as possible. Now imagine what your life would look like if either this stressor were removed or you no longer felt the same levels of stress. What would it be like?

WRITE DOWN AT LEAST THREE THINGS THAT WOULD BE
DIFFERENT IF YOU WERE ABLE TO QUIETEN YOUR STRESS
RESPONSE TO THIS PARTICULAR STIMULANT.

1. ....

....

....

2. ....

....

....

3. ....

....

....

....

WHAT YOU ARE LOOKING FOR IS WHAT IS LOOKING

Having recognised the negative effects of stress, fear, and the amygdala hijack—and the need to harness our adaptability—the temptation is to jump straight in with the AQ model. However, if we do that, then we are only feeding the fear response, not overcoming it. The subtitle of this segment, "What you are looking for is what is looking", is a quote from St. Francis of Assisi that, to my mind, deftly illustrates the power of observation to break the negative cycles we so often get trapped in.

As we navigate from fear to fact, we must first transition our thinking.

In the context of work, our jobs and our roles are linked to our identities. In fact, it is probably the second question you ask when you meet someone new. After "what's your name?", you will likely ask, "so what do you do?" This simple act often locks us in, and when there is a need to evolve, to step out from a past role, we often become defensive and protective, holding onto the things we hold true about who we are. To begin to imagine a new future self, to take the first steps in leveraging your adaptability intelligence, your AQ, I practise a 3-step process for harnessing AQ as a leader.

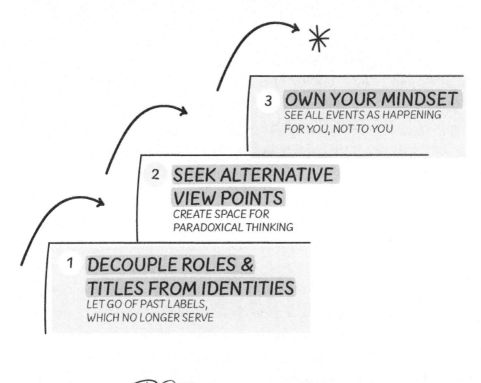

3 STEPS TO HARNESS AQ AS A LEADER

3 OWN YOUR MINDSET
SEE ALL EVENTS AS HAPPENING
FOR YOU, NOT TO YOU

**2 SEEK ALTERNATIVE
VIEW POINTS**
CREATE SPACE FOR
PARADOXICAL THINKING

**1 DECOUPLE ROLES &
TITLES FROM IDENTITIES**
LET GO OF PAST LABELS,
WHICH NO LONGER SERVE

Ross Thornley

THE **AQ** GUY

AQai.

1. Decouple Roles & Titles From Identity (let go of labels)

2. Seek Alternative Viewpoints (create space for paradoxical thinking)

3. Own Your Mindset (see events as happening for you not to you)

All of these stages are interlinked and reinforce one another. It might also be the case that you find one easier than the other. We'll start with this process of *decoupling*.

The English poet John Keats observed a certain property or trait in highly successful people which he termed "Negative Capability" when a person is: "... capable of being in uncertainties, mysteries, doubts, without any irritable reaching after fact and reason."[5] The American writer F. Scott Fitzgerald, author of *The Great Gatsby*, corroborated this idea in his work by proposing, "The test of a first-rate intelligence is the ability to hold two opposed ideas in mind at the same time and still retain the ability to function."

In other words, it is not about what we *do* in response to "uncertainties, mysteries, doubts" but rather about not allowing the fear-response to take over. We are able to simply *be*, to reside in the uncertainty without feeling the need to compensate—to fight or flee. Now, this is obviously very difficult to achieve, and it may take us some time to work up to this level of an almost transcendent state. The first step, however, is to decouple ourselves from *our* fear, aka, from our emotions. I should stress at the start that I am not advocating for complete detachment, or that you make yourself into a kind of machine. The trick is to recognise what emotions really are so that when required you can shift to a place of observation rather than identification.

The language we use around emotions is very peculiar and very revealing of how we process identity. We say, *"I'm angry."* Not, "I'm experiencing anger." We say, *"I'm upset."* Not, "I'm experiencing sadness." Because we *identify* with our emotions, making them synonymous with the "I", we enthrone the emotions as our "Self", when in fact they are not the true Self. When we do this, we give emotions power over us, because we have mistakenly claimed they *are* us. This mostly unconscious act is neuro-linguistic programming but of the negative kind.

However, if we can decouple from the emotional state and recognise it as just that: a state, then we can begin to move towards "Negative Capability", acceptance of the reality without the need to change it. When we begin to explore the "true Self" we move towards almost mystical territory, and this is because the discovery of the true Self, the observer within, leads to awesome empowerment. St. Francis of Assisi said, "What you are looking for is what is looking." When we become observers of our emotions we diminish their control over us and reclaim our ability to engage the higher thinking brain (rather than being "hijacked" by the reptilian brain). This allows us to see through the illusions our thoughts and feelings create.

To share a personal example, I recently experienced a very difficult period in my life in which I became overwhelmed by the sheer volume of traumatic experiences that seemed to be piling up on me one after another (both good and bad things always seem to arrive in herds, don't they?). During this time, I took the opportunity to reflect on my life and my feelings, what was not serving me in the vision I hold for myself, and how I needed to shift my perspective and accept what was in front of me.

The period of reflection came when I fell sick with a sore throat, persistent headache, and runny eyes and nose. This was unusual for me, as I tend to be a high-energy, healthy person. I'm known as an optimist in all my social circles, yet accompanying my physical dis-ease was a feeling of total overwhelm. My usual "habit" when sick is to dive back into work as soon as the symptoms begin to alleviate. I had calls, collaborations, and podcast interviews all lined up. I didn't want to let anyone down. But I simply could not face it, and decided to take a few days off.

All my Covid-19 tests were negative. Despite the mental fog, I realised this sickness was something else. In fact, my physical illness was most likely a build-up from a series of traumatic events giving a bashing to my immune system.

In 2021, my father was given three to six months to live with stage-4 lung cancer. My wife was also diagnosed with cancer in the same few weeks. Thankfully, as I write this, my Dad is still here and has transformed his life with amazing progress and some radical remission results. And my wife is doing well, after recovering from surgery and several treatments. But this doesn't take away from the impact and stress of the diagnosis for all of us.

In the same few months, I broke my elbow and a couple of ribs, from a fall whilst building a new home office and yoga room, reducing my range of movement to about 30 degrees. It's surprising how many activities become difficult when you lose movement and range.

My previous business, which I sold after 18 successful and profitable years, went into liquidation eighteen months after I sold it, and a personal guarantee came back to bite me which could have resulted in losing my house.

My resilience muscle had a good workout during those twelve months. And whilst my body shouted for help in the throes of illness, I ended up feeling blessed and strong for the future.

I realised I had the skills, support, and confidence that not only would we survive, but flourish as a result of these events. The following framework might help you if you are going through something similar:

To be aware, and notice my thoughts and feelings.

That I am an observer of them.

To acknowledge emotion is energy passing through the body

To see my thoughts as thoughts. And not see the situation through them.

To accept difficult feelings, allowing them to come and pass.

To commit to what I care about, and to take action to move me closer to what matters most.

Just know that as with all things in life, It will pass.

As you can see, decoupling from our emotions is easier said than done, especially when we are going through difficult periods in our life. However, it is only by doing this that we can create sufficient peace of mind to seek alternative viewpoints, which is the next stage in the 3-step model of harnessing AQ. We will cover this in more detail later in the book, as well as stage 3, transforming our mindset to see events as happening *for* us rather than *to* us. If this sounds like a lot to take in, please don't worry, as we will return to these themes and unpack them in greater depth.

To summarise, all the above factors: amygdala hijacking, our rapidly changing environment, our difficulty dealing with uncertainties, our biological limitations which prevent us from differentiating between the life-threatening and the uncertain, societal conditioning which prevents dissipation of built-up stress, and self-identification with our emotions— **MEAN WE MASSIVELY CURTAIL OUR AMBITIONS.** It's very difficult to believe great things are possible when we are in a "survival mindset". Indeed, in the Hierarchy of Needs, Maslow theorised that only if the basic "physiological" (aka survival) needs were met could we begin to ascend the pyramid towards secondary needs and finally transcendence where we attend to the needs of others. Of course, as I mentioned before, Maslow's model is largely out of date despite resonating with a wide audience even to this day, which is why I have created our adaptable alternative to the Pyramid of Needs.

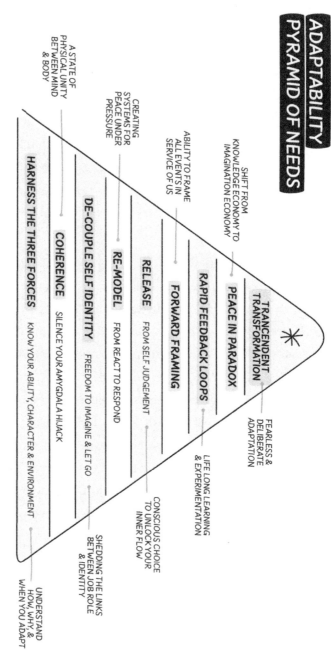

ADAPTABILITY PYRAMID OF NEEDS

THE **AQ** GUY

TRANCENDENT TRANSFORMATION — FEARLESS & DELIBERATE ADAPTATION

SHIFT FROM KNOWLEDGE ECONOMY TO IMAGINATION ECONOMY

PEACE IN PARADOX — LIFE LONG LEARNING & EXPERIMENTATION

ABILITY TO FRAME ALL EVENTS IN SERVICE OF US

RAPID FEEDBACK LOOPS — CONSCIOUS CHOICE TO UNLOCK YOUR INNER FLOW

CREATING SYSTEMS FOR PEACE UNDER PRESSURE

FORWARD FRAMING

RELEASE — FROM SELF JUDGEMENT

RE-MODEL — FROM REACT TO RESPOND

A STATE OF PHYSICAL UNITY BETWEEN MIND & BODY

DE-COUPLE SELF IDENTITY — FREEDOM TO IMAGINE & LET GO

COHERENCE — SILENCE YOUR AMYGDALA HIJACK

SHEDDING THE LINKS BETWEEN JOB ROLE & IDENTITY

HARNESS THE THREE FORCES — KNOW YOUR ABILITY, CHARACTER & ENVIRONMENT

UNDERSTAND HOW, WHY, & WHEN YOU ADAPT

AQai.

We will be unpacking the nine levels of the Adaptability Pyramid of Needs™ as we progress throughout this book. Suffice to say, adaptability is the key to unlocking our ability to transcend, to harness our maximum potential, transforming us from reactive individuals into inspiring leaders. We start by "observing" rather than reacting with a fear response to stimuli. This allows us to **DECOUPLE FROM SELF-IDENTIFICATION WITH OUR EMOTIONS AND THINK MORE CLEARLY.**

From here, we can forge greater control and direction in our lives. When I say "control" that doesn't mean micromanaging every minute aspect of our day-to-day existence; it means feeling empowered to achieve our wildest dreams and regaining the confidence to stretch our ambitions rather than "settle". Many businesses and self-help books talk about SMART goals, and whilst I believe specificity and measurability are important—as well as a due date to galvanise you towards achieving the goal—I think that words like "Achievable" and "Realistic" set a cap on our ambition. These words are the fear response talking again: "What if I fail?", "What if I can't do it?", "No one has ever done it before, so why do I think I can?" In a world powered by exponential technology, even the sky is not the limit.

Not only this, but ambition is not static. If we "accomplish" our ambitions, we are no longer moving forward. Goals can be accomplished, but ambitions are continual. It is the old adage that those who retire early seem to die early unless they don't really retire at all but actually leave work to pursue some other ambition such as writing a memoir or creating the garden of their dreams. In other words, our goalposts *should* move, because as we grow and develop our ideas, correspondingly our ambitions change and evolve too.

This *is* adaptability.

EXERCISE 4:

TAKE A LOOK AT THE ADAPTABILITY PYRAMID OF NEEDS™, ARE THERE AREAS THAT RESONATE WITH YOU?

WHERE DO YOU THINK YOU STRUGGLE MOST?

Reflect on what this model reveals to you.

SUMMARY FOR PART 1

→ THE FUTURE BELONGS TO THOSE WHO TRAIN THEIR ADAPTABILITY MUSCLE

→ OUR SPECIES HAS ADAPTED TO ITS CIRCUMSTANCES AND ENVIRONMENT MORE THAN ANY OTHER ON THE PLANET, AND YET BIOLOGICALLY WE HAVE CHANGED VERY LITTLE

→ THE BRAIN HAS A TENDENCY TO HOLD ON TO NEGATIVE MEMORIES OR FEELINGS. THIS IS OUR NEGATIVE COGNITIVE BIAS

→ STRESS LITERALLY "SHRINKS" OUR BRAINS

→ THE ESSENTIAL STEPS TO TRAIN YOUR ADAPTABILITY MUSCLE, AND EXPAND SELF-MASTERY ARE TO
A. DECOUPLE OURSELVES FROM OUR FEAR,
B. OUR CURRENT IDENTITIES, AND
C. OUR EMOTIONS. AS WE BECOME OBSERVERS OF SELF.

1 Ryan, M. J., *AdaptAbility*; Broadway Books; 2009.
2 Kahneman D, Frederick S (2002). "Representativeness Revisited: Attribute Substitution in Intuitive Judgment". In Gilovich T, Griffin DW, Kahneman D (eds.). *Heuristics and Biases: The Psychology of Intuitive Judgment*. Cambridge: Cambridge University Press. pp. 51–52.
3 Psychologies Magazine; *Real Strength*; Capstone; 2017.
4 The example was quoted in *Brand Failures* by Matt Haig.
5 Li, Ou; Keats and Negative Capability; Continuum International Publishing Group; 2009; p.ix.

PART 2: THE AQ MODEL

KNOW THE ENEMY & OPPORTUNITY

Companies are made up of people and their thinking. They are symbiotic beings composed of tens, hundreds, sometimes even thousands of different organisms. They are the collective result of months, years, decades—sometimes even centuries—of ideas from all the people who have ever passed through their doors. The success of an organisation is determined by their collective thinking being appropriate to the time and environment. In *Moonshot Innovation*, I discussed a number of historical organisations that introduced brilliant, innovative concepts to the market but at the wrong time and so subsequently failed. In life, as in business, everything is contextual to now. That is why adaptability is so vitally important because it teaches us how to become one with the now and to become one with our environment, not fight against it.

Leaders must now steer their organisations through a VUCA (volatile, uncertain, complex, ambiguous) world. According to the U.S. Bureau of Labour Statistics, some **47.4 MILLION PEOPLE VOLUNTARILY LEFT THEIR JOBS IN 2021.**

In December 2021, there were a reported **58 UNEMPLOYED WORKERS FOR EVERY 100 JOB OPENINGS—THAT'S NEARLY TWO JOBS FOR EVERY PERSON LOOKING FOR ONE.**[1]

In other words, there's plenty of employment, contrary to the scaremongering, but there's either an unwillingness to do it, a lack of skills, or better opportunities elsewhere (such as self-employment). This is a deficit organisations will have to address, and quickly.

Over the last 2 years, I've had hundreds of conversations and personally interviewed over 90 coaches, HR leaders, and entrepreneurs from around the world on my podcast, *Decoding AQ*, and many fear displacement in our age, and with good reason. It's estimated 1,000,000 jobs will vanish in the US by 2026[2], and 800 million worldwide by 2030[3], saying nothing of the potential billions that will need to be re-skilled into new roles. In fact, many have already been displaced. U.S. auto manufacturing jobs dropped from 1.3 million in 2000 to 942,000 in June 2017, a loss of 358,000 jobs[4]. And all of this displacement happened three years *before* Covid-19, which has caused further disruption to the "normal".

This is the environment we inhabit. And this environment is also changing minute by minute. What does this mean in the context of adapting in our careers, or adapting in our workforces, teams, and organisations? Historically, we could spend many years testing and figuring stuff out, and the consequences weren't death: companies were immensely secure. **TODAY, THE AVERAGE AGE OF AN S&P 500 COMPANY IS UNDER 20 YEARS, DOWN FROM 60 YEARS IN THE 1950S, ACCORDING TO CREDIT SUISSE.** Now, if we fail to rapidly and continually adapt and experiment, and fail to find new solutions for market fit, it seems like the consequences are fatal no matter how big the organisation is.

I recognise these are not just statistics, but people and families who will now have to rapidly adapt and find a new way to live, which is not to be underestimated. Many will have to learn new skills as their old skills become redundant with changing processes. Consider how typing was once a skill that you could wear on your CV. By contrast, we will soon see an age where most aspects of advanced accountancy and even legal services will be fully automated. It's not robots that will take our jobs, it's software that's eating job tasks. The enemy here is not 'change', per se.

THE ENEMY IS THE SPEED OF EXPANDING COMPLEXITY, BUT THE COM-

PLEXITY IS ALSO THE OPPORTUNITY.

In defining the skills people will need in the future world of work, research published in June 2021 by McKinsey Global Institute surveyed 18,000 people across 15 countries, which identified 56 foundational skills that will help people thrive.

These distinct skills and attitudes were termed "DELTAs" rather than skills because they were a mix of both skills and attitudes. Most interestingly, when holding all variables constant—including demographic variables and proficiency in all other elements—they identified employment was most strongly associated with proficiency in several DELTAs within the self-leadership category, namely "adaptability," "coping with uncertainty," "synthesizing messages," and "achievement orientation".

PROFICIENCY IN CERTAIN FACTORS* IS LINKED WITH HIGHER LIKELIHOOD OF EMPLOYMENT

A SURVEY OF 18,000 PEOPLE IN 15 COUNTRIES
INCREASED CHANCE OF RESPONDENTS WITH A HIGHER PROFICIENCY IN THE DELTA[1] BEING EMPLOYED[2] %

ADAPTABILITY

COPING WITH UNCERTAINTY

SYNTHESIZING MESSAGES

ACHIEVEMENT ORIENTATION

FOSTERING INCLUSIVENESS

ENERGY, PASSION, AND OPTIMISM

UNDERSTANDING OWN STRENGTHS

DIGITAL COLLABORATION

SMART SYSTEMS

SELF-CONTROL & REGULATION

24 **18** **12** **11** **9** **9** **8** **8** **7** **7**

*FACTORS - CALLED DELTAs IN THE RESEARCH - BECAUSE THEY ARE A MIX OF SKILLS AND ATTITUDES
NOTE: THE MARGIN OF ERROR IS 3% WITH A 95% CONFIDENCE INTERVAL. DELTAs SELECTED
BASED ON INDIVIDUAL CONTRIBUTION - HOLDING OTHER VARIABLES CONSTANT - THE THE
PROBABILITY OF A SURVEY PARTICIPANT BEING EMPLOYED AMONG THOSE WITH INCOME BELOW
MEDIAN OR THOSE WITH NO INCOME. PEOPLE WITH INCOME ABOVE THE MEDIAN WERE EXCLUDED
TO AVOID SKEWED RESULTS BECAUSE OF HIGHER PROFICIENCY IN DELTAs.

1. DISTINCT ELEMENT OF TALNET
2. INCREASE IN THE ODDS OF BEING EMPLOYED IF PROFICIENCY SCORE IS HIGHER BY 1 LEVEL,
   ASSUMING ALL OTHER ELEMENTS AND DEMOGRAPHIC VARIABLES ARE FIXED/CONSTANT.
   ONLY OECD CONTRIES INCLUDED IN THIS ANALYSIS.

 THE **AQ** GUY

SOURCE: McKINSEY & COMPANY   5

In simple terms:

HIGHER ADAPTABILITY LEADS TO HIGHER LEVELS OF EMPLOYMENT.

Not only that, but **Daniel Goleman** the 'father of EQ', observed

"OF ALL OF THE EMOTIONAL INTELLIGENCE COMPETENCIES, STRENGTH IN ADAPTABILITY PREDICTS SUCCESS MOST OFTEN."

Adaptability is not only the solution, therefore, for individuals seeking work, but also for organisations seeking success.

HOW, WHY, AND WHEN WE ADAPT

Adaptability has been called the "new competitive advantage" by Harvard Business School, was among the top five soft skills sought by employers according to the 2019 LinkedIn Global Trends study[6], and was the number one skill sought after by Learning & Development professionals in 2021 according to LinkedIn's Workforce Learning report.

Research, science, and simple observations from life experience show us each person adapts in a different way for different reasons. Whilst earlier I broadly described some of the qualities of adaptability, adaptability is not "one thing": it is contextual. Therefore, in order to truly understand adaptability, and to harness it for the benefit of our people and teams, our organisations—and yes ourselves too!—we have to ask three foundational questions:

→ **HOW PEOPLE ADAPT?**

→ **WHY PEOPLE ADAPT?**

→ **AND WHEN PEOPLE ADAPT?**

This, in turn, will allow us to predict who is likely to adapt in a given circumstance, and indeed, the data we have collected is already revealing observable trends, which we will share with you later.

EXERCISE 5:

Think for a moment about these three fundamental questions.

Reflect and write down your answer in a couple of sentences.

WHY DO YOU ADAPT?

....

....

....

....

....

HOW DO YOU ADAPT?

....

....

....

....

(do you throw everything out and start again or tweak what you did before)?

And lastly,

WHEN DO YOU ADAPT

....

....

....

....

(what might be the environmental triggers)?

Adaptability is part of the natural world, our evolution, and the evolution of the environments we create around us, but one interesting thing about this is that the natural world can actually benefit from our interference (as well, of course, as being hampered by us and our lack of environmental consideration). When we interact with nature in a wholesome way, pruning our gardens, they flourish anew. When we temper growth in certain areas, it causes a massive growth in others. I compare this to the issue of being able to let go of past successes. A certain branch may have been helpful in the past, but now it's hurting the core, so we have to prune it, to let go of it, in order to flourish again. This is going to be one of the biggest challenges we see in the workplace of the future.

It's as much about what we're going to have to unlearn as learn.

To continue the thread of evolution: just as our society shifted from valuing IQ (intelligence quotient) to valuing EQ (emotional intelligence), we are now seeing a shift from EQ to AQ (adaptability quotient), although arguably, I believe the latter in fact encompasses both of the former!

IQ is defined as:

"THE ABILITY TO REASON, PLAN, SOLVE PROBLEMS, THINK ABSTRACTLY, COMPREHEND COMPLEX IDEAS, LEARN QUICKLY AND LEARN FROM EXPERIENCE."

EQ as:

"THE CAPABILITY TO BE AWARE OF, CONTROL, AND EXPRESS ONE'S EMOTIONS, AND TO HANDLE INTERPERSONAL RELATIONSHIPS JUDICIOUSLY AND EMPATHETICALLY."

Adaptability, on the other hand,

"IS THE CAPACITY TO ADJUST ONE'S THOUGHTS AND BEHAVIOURS IN ORDER TO EFFECTIVELY RESPOND TO UNCERTAINTY, NEW INFORMATION, OR CHANGED CIRCUMSTANCES."[7]

We see this definition of adaptability establishes a link between thoughts and behaviours, between processing information and acting upon it, and between the "soft" skills of emotional and environmental awareness versus harder skills such as problem-solving (aka, the ability to "effectively respond").

AQ (adaptability quotient) is not just a fad or a trend, though it is rising to prominence. Our adaptability has always been a defining factor of who we are and our survival right up until this point in time.

Adaptability is not just about survival, however. It is also about thriving. As David Green observed in his book *The Age of Wellbeing*, "I still believe there is more of a focus on problems and survival rather than opportunities and thriving." This correlates to the negative cognitive bias all human beings have been indoctrinated into. We can see adaptability as purely a survival tool, to merely "get by", or we can start looking at it as an opportunity to do more than we ever dreamed.

When looking at the most successful organisations and individuals in the world, the one commonality I have observed they all shared, the thing distinguishing them from their competitors, was adaptability. This wasn't just a factor in who "made the cut" but who actively turned their setbacks into profitability, purposeful positive action, and success. Observing this success factor led me to co-found AQai with Mike Raven, an organisation dedicated to unlocking the secrets of human adaptability, to inspire and empower every human with the skills to adapt and thrive, ensuring no one is left behind in the fastest period of change in history.

With the driving forces of accelerated change, and the desire to expand the understanding of our behaviour, neuroscience, and our ability to navigate and thrive amidst our VUCA world, we set about developing the first-ever holistic and scientifically valid metric of AQ.

So, how do we actually define and measure AQ?

Like many of the most important things in life we want to improve, it all starts with the ability to accurately measure and report progress. If we can't measure our motivation, productivity, our emotional health, we are simply stabbing in the dark. It can often be very difficult to quantify these ambiguous concepts in a metric, numerical way, but that is the process of science. As Galileo observed, "This grand book of the universe... is written in the language of mathematics, and its characters are triangles, circles, and other geometric figures without which it is humanly impossible to understand a single word of it; without these, one wanders about in a dark labyrinth."

We have spent years collating the highest level of peer-reviewed studies, the established and the latest research, and observing cutting-edge trends to formulate our comprehensive operating system for adaptability. From this, we understand AQ in terms of three interrelated inputs, three master dimensions if you will:

- **Ability** (your adaptability skills - **How** and to what degree one adapts)

This is your adaption muscle system. It reflects how, over time, you can develop mastery in multiple or changing fields. This element encompasses your ability to be resilient and bounce back/or even forward from hardship, mental flexibility with holding opposing thoughts, your grit, as well as your mindset and ability to unlearn.

- **Character** (**who** adapts and **why**)

This reflects a more innate (but contextual) aspect of adaptability quotient: most broadly we can call it "the way you tick": what drives you, what frames of mind you operate by, and your styles of working. Together with your likely willingness to adapt. Whilst you may be able to live with other characteristics in specific circumstances, we seek to understand preferences which channel flow and not compliance when it comes to why someone makes an adaptation of change. This important master dimension uncovers your profile in motivation style, emotional range, extraversion, thinking style and hope.

- **Environment** (how your environment can help or hinder your adaption - **When** one adapts, and to what degree)

Your environment can either help or inhibit your adaption. This can typically be out of your control, yet you are part of the input! We explore areas such as company support, team support (psychological safety), work environment, emotional health, and work stress.

These three master dimensions further break down into seventeen sub-dimensions, which allows us to drill down into specifics.

This creates what we call our "**AQ Adaptiotic Table**™".

THE A.C.E MODEL OF ADAPTABILITY

THE 17 SCIENTIFICALLY VALID MEASURES OF ADAPTABILITY

AQ ABILITY

HOW AND TO WHAT DEGREE DO I ADAPT?

1. GRIT
2. MENTAL FLEXIBILITY
3. MINDSET
4. RESILIENCE
5. UNLEARN

AQ CHARACTER

WHO ADAPTS AND **WHY?**

6. EMOTIONAL RANGE
7. EXTRAVERSION
8. HOPE
9. MOTIVATION STYLE
10. THINKING STYLE

AQ ENVIRONMENT

WHEN DOES SOMEONE ADAPT TO WHAT DEGREE?

11. COMPANY SUPPORT
12. EMOTIONAL HEALTH
13. TEAM SUPPORT
14. WORK ENVIRONMENT
15. WORK STRESS

AI PREDICTIVE INDEXES

16. CHANGE READINESS INDEX
17. RESKILL INDEX

THE AQ GUY

AQai.

We collaborated with Dr Nicholas T. Deuschel, a research professor at Spain's leading Carlos III University and used one of the most robust models in organisational psychology (the input-process-outcome model) to create our tripartite Ability Character Environment model (or A.C.E.). In our case "adaptability" is the outcome, a result of a process and an input.

In our model, AQ-Character fuels adaption (this is the "input"). In other words, extraversion-introversion, our motivation style, and our "personality traits", all create the impetus that drives us to adapt. This certainly does not mean that if you have a certain character type you won't be able to adapt or change. To the contrary! Building on dozens of studies in psychology and business, as well as our own research, we have found AQ-Character establishes why we adapt in the first place.

At the same time employees can learn new skills that allow them to adapt in different ways. This is AQ-Ability which also adds to the "input" stage of the model.

In addition, we are also influenced by our environment. We may have all the unique skills in the world to help us adapt, even a personality that is innately adaptable, but due to an inhibiting environment are unable to fully harness our AQ muscle. This is also another important "input".

We then experience the "process" in the form of adaptability behaviours, such as exploration (to seek out new and different ideas, and ways of doing things), exploitation (to utilise and maximise current resources and approaches), problem-solving, and creativity. And in a business context these manifest in a series of outputs: desired, predicted, and actual "outcomes". For example accelerated innovation, employee engagement, retention and reskilling with increased employee mobility and dynamic career pathways, learning and development culture, overall productivity and performance, together with health and wellbeing—stress and burnout reduction.

Understanding the specific flow, mix and value of inputs, the resulting and chosen processes and then the impact on outcomes will help us to continually leverage and optimise what we understand as our adaptability intelligence. It is also important to consider the loop effect, where many 'outputs' become feed-back data points as future inputs too!

INPUT

AQ ABILITY
GRIT
MENTAL FLEXIBILITY
MINDSET
RESILIENCE
UNLEARN

AQ CHARACTER
EMOTIONAL RANGE
EXTRAVERSION
HOPE
MOTIVATION STYLE
THINKING STYLE

AQ ENVIRONMENT
COMPANY SUPPORT
EMOTIONAL HEALTH
TEAM SUPPORT
WORK ENVIRONMENT
WORK STRESS

PROCESS

ADAPTABILITY BEHAVIOURS

EXPLORE & TRANSFORM
EXPLOITATION - UTILIZE & IMPROVE
PROBLEM-SOLVING
CREATIVITY
COMMUNICATION LEVELS
LEADERSHIP STYLES
PRACTICES & PROCEDURES
SPEED OF LEARNING
DECISION MAKING
PRO-ACTIVE
REACTIVE

OUTPUT

ACCELERATED INNOVATION
PROFITABILITY
RELEVANCE
EMPLOYEE ENGAGEMENT
RETENTION
RESKILLING
EMPLOYEE MOBILITY
DYNAMIC CAREER PATHWAYS
LEARNING AND DEVELOPMENT
CULTURE
PRODUCTIVITY & PERFORMANCE
MENTAL HEALTH
WELLBEING, STRESS, BURNOUT
COLLAPSE / THRIVING

EXAMPLES OF THE INPUT, PROCESS, OUTPUT MODEL IN RELATION TO ADAPTABILITY

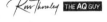 THE **AQ** GUY

AQai.

AQ ABILITY

First, we will focus on AQ-Ability. Whilst we understand AQ in terms of three master dimensions, we believe

AQ-ABILITY—WHICH IS LEARNABLE AND CAN EVOLVE—CAN HAVE THE GREATEST IMPACT ON OUR ADAPTABILITY.

We have identified five key sub-dimensions of our AQ-Ability. These sub-dimensions were selected based on their frequent intersection across all the studies we examined.

Before we get into the specific sub-dimensions, let's first explore the career construction model of adaptability which identifies the following three traits of adaptability:

→ **ADAPTS READILY TO CHANGING RULES**

→ **STRIVES TO LEARN NEW PROCESSES**

→ **IS OPEN TO NEW WAYS OF DOING THINGS**[8]

Pairing these findings with Scott Keller and Colin Price's work, along with many other intersectional studies, we found AQ-Ability to be comprised of the following:

→ **GRIT (OUR ABILITY TO 'STAY THE COURSE', TO FOLLOW THROUGH WHEN APPROACHING IMPORTANT GOALS.)**

→ **MENTAL FLEXIBILITY (THE ABILITY TO ACCEPT, APPRECIATE, AND**

EMBRACE COMPETING DEMANDS OR PROBLEMS.)

→ MINDSET (SPECIFICALLY OUR RELATIONSHIP WITH CHANGE, AND OUR PREDICTIONS OF POSITIVE OR NEGATIVE OUTCOMES)

→ RESILIENCE (OUR ABILITY TO RECOVER QUICKLY FROM DIFFICULTIES & SET-BACKS, OR, IN OTHER WORDS, THE ABILITY TO 'BOUNCE BACK' OR 'BOUNCE-FORWARD'.)

→ UNLEARNING (THE ABILITY TO INTENTIONALLY "LET GO" OF PREVIOUS KNOWLEDGE. TO REASSESS BASED ON NEW AND OLD DATA.)

Understanding these aspects and how they interact will help us improve and transform our own adaptability, guiding us away from systems collapse and survival, and supporting us towards thriving and perpetual growth.

Let's dig deeper into AQ-Ability and specifically the five sub-dimensions.

1. GRIT

Grit is our ability to "stay the course", to follow through on our long-term objectives. This is not to be conflated with Resilience, which is our ability to bounce back, or indeed bounce forward from setbacks. Grit is another kind of fortitude.

As hypothesised by Duckworth & Seligman in 2007, Grit is the **passion** (that is the consistency of interest) and **perseverance** (this is the persistence of effort) to pursue those longer-term goals. Angela Duckworth's book, titled *Grit* is a great study and dives into the science of Grit.

If we think of Grit in this way, it is the mental toughness, the mental stamina to keep going, to stick with an undertaking in spite of difficulties, obstacles, or discouragement in order to achieve a long-term goal. Often higher when aligned with one's interest or passion.

Studies have distinguished Grit from Resilience. Grit entails consistency of interests and goals over time, whereas the construct of resilience is "agnostic" on the stability of an individual's interests. Grit also differs from leadership potential insofar as the arenas in which "gritty" individuals demonstrate their stamina need not be those that entail organising and managing other people. Likewise, Grit can be distinguished from conscientiousness, a multi-dimensional family of personality traits that encompasses perseverance but also includes tendencies toward responsibility, self-control, orderliness, and traditionalism[9]. While correlated with conscientiousness, Grit provides incremental predictive validity for achievement outcomes, particularly in settings of high challenge.

Some 130 years ago, Galton collected biographical information on the top achievers of his time. From judges, statesmen, scientists, poets, musicians and many others. Seeking to identify any common attributes or traits to correlate to their success. He concluded ability alone did not result in their achievement. He believed the top performers had three key aspects, "ability combined with zeal and with capacity for hard labour" (p.33). These conclusions have been repeated throughout history, with Cox (1926) who analysed 301 eminent creators and leaders drawn from a sample compiled by J. M. Cattell (1903). When the rank order of this list was plotted against estimated IQ, there was only moderate relation (r.16). When Cox ranked these high achievers against the 67 character traits derived from Webb (1915), he concluded that holding constant estimated IQ, when "persistence of motive and effort, confidence in their abilities and great strength or force of character" was seen in childhood it was the greatest prediction of lifetime achievement.

The powerful mix of Grit and Resilience has a critical impact on future performance, success and achievement. Both are essential components of our adaptability intelligence. However, please note Grit is not a personality trait as previously thought, but a learnable skill. We can develop our Grit over time in the same way as we can other "soft" skills. Angela L. Duckworth from the University of Pennsylvania, also discovered that Grit increases with age. The same trend has been revealed from our thousands of AQme assessments over the last 4 years.

It is important to always consider the setting and objectives, to really under-stand the advantages or disadvantages of certain scores and levels of ability proficiency. Having low Grit can even be an advantage in some circumstances.

LOW GRIT

"I WANT TO DO SOMETHING ELSE, I QUIT"

→ Unable to stick to long-term goals

→ Have projects often left unfinished

→ Switch tasks often

→ Give up difficult tasks quickly

→ Be easily discouraged

→ Find it difficult to stay on course

MEDIUM GRIT

"I WILL KEEP GOING, BUT I NEED HELP"

→ Be able to reach long-term goals

→ Look for multiple ways to achieve a task

→ Show commitment and 'keep working at it'

→ Benefit from support to finish tasks

→ Put off or delay tasks

→ Can avoid tasks when lacking passion

HIGH GRIT

"I'VE GOT THIS AND WILL DO WHATEVER IT TAKES"

→ Confident in achieving long term goals

→ Described as 'determined' and 'hard working'

→ Have a high capacity to persevere

→ **Known to finish what you start**

→ **Often stick to a plan**

→ **Not easily be discouraged**

2. MENTAL FLEXIBILITY

Flexibility is defined by OED as "the quality of bending easily without breaking." This brings to mind the Bruce Lee quote I shared earlier, "You must be shapeless, formless, like water."

Carl Jung once said, "What resists, persists." In other words, the more we reject something, the worse we make it for ourselves. A metaphorical example of this might be trying to stay afloat in the ocean. If you kick hard treading water, sooner than you think you will succumb to exhaustion, unable to keep your head above water. However, if you adjust your posture, relax, lie on your back, and try to simply float on the water, you might be able to stay there a good long while! Change and new information trigger our fear response which is aptly symbolised in this desperate need to tread water, but if we go *with* the change and relax, we find we are carried along by the tide.

Mental Flexibility is the ability to observe the current, to see things for what they are, together with the ability to create new pathways, to change them with effective action, if indeed you choose it necessary to do so. Dr Michael Sinclar defines psychological flexibility as, "The ability to contact your present moment experience, without defence, as fully as possible as a conscious human being. To change or persist in behaviour so you can move towards the stuff you really care about in life; what you value. To be mindfully aware of thoughts and feelings and to commit to value-based living".

In their research paper "Transitioning Towards New Ways of Working: Do Job Demands, Job Resources, Burnout, and Engagement Change?", Elianne F. Van Steenbergen, Cilia van der Ven, Maria C. W. Peeters, and Toon W. Taris outlined the factors that may help to transition to new modes of work, in one example, telecommuting: "Judge, Thoresen, Pucik, and Welbourne (1999) found that

MANAGERS HIGHER IN OPENNESS TO EXPERIENCES WERE BETTER ABLE TO COPE WITH ORGANISATIONAL CHANGE.

Moreover, practical personal resources such as flexibility (i.e., adapting to changes at work)... may enable employees to make an optimal transition to telecommuting. (Lapierre et al., 2015)."

In our AQ model and context, Mental flexibility refers to the ability to

ACCEPT, APPRECIATE, AND EMBRACE COMPETING DEMANDS OR PROBLEMS.

It allows one to see tensions or trade-offs in everyday or business life as opportunities, opportunities that allow innovative ways to learn and ultimately adapt.

What is often referred to as organisational flexibility is the ability to pursue both exploratory and exploitative innovations[10], and has been shown to be important for organisational prosperity and survival[11].

Exploration results from experimentation, flexibility, and divergent thinking. Exploitation is associated with efficiency, refinement, and focus, and with achieving higher reliability by refining existing competencies. Exploration results in increasing variety by searching for and experimenting with new opportunities. Both are key in individual, team, and organisational adaptability.

Researchers have argued that both types of innovation behaviours and learning activities are essential for the effective functioning and enduring viability of an organisation[12]. Therefore your employees and teams must conduct both routine and nonroutine activities, fulfil administrative and entrepreneurial roles, and combine short- and long-term views. Living often in a paradox, which is a tough call!

In simple terms, one might describe this as "**open-mindedness**". But it is much more than this. With great mental flexibility comes a deliberate act of pursuing opposing behaviours, thoughts, and actions to expand the propensity for greater success through continual adaptative experiments.

However, it is important to be aware of our own various biases we have picked up over time. Some obvious, some less obvious. In terms of how this links to our level of mental flexibility, well, we may believe we are open-minded, but in actuality are still operating within our own comfort zone and the existing constraints of what we believe. In reality, we are blind to that which exists outside this space of the perceived familiar.

→ ARE WE TRULY STEPPING OUTSIDE OF OUR ECHO CHAMBER AND PREPARED TO SEE ALTERNATIVE POINTS OF VIEW?

→ ARE YOU DRAINED OR ENERGISED BY COMPETING DEMANDS?

→ CAN YOU HOLD TWO OPPOSING THOUGHTS IN YOUR MIND AND REMAIN SANE?

→ IMPORTANTLY ARE YOU ABLE TO HOLD THESE THOUGHTS FOR JUST A SHORT PERIOD, OR CAN YOU DO THIS OVER A LONG TIME? AND CAN YOU REPEATEDLY EXPLOIT EXISTING KNOWLEDGE AND

PURSUE AND EXPLORE NEW WAYS OF DOING THINGS, TIME AND TIME AGAIN?

One way to think of this is: It is the ability to be in love with the problem rather than the solution, and to remain open to alternative methods, approaches, and ideas.

LOW MENTAL FLEXIBILITY

"I HAVEN'T GOT TIME TO FIND A NEW WAY"

→ Workplace problems resurface often

→ Constantly feel 'up against it'

→ Hard to manage competing demands

→ Prefer to pursue one single goal

→ Good at following a single plan route

→ Less open to new ideas

MEDIUM MENTAL FLEXIBILITY

"THAT SOUNDS INTERESTING, TELL ME MORE"

→ Ability to 'deal with' competing demands

→ Work on multiple & contradictory tasks

→ Open to new perspectives

→ Conflicting goals can be draining

→ Adapts approach depending on environment

→ Is aware and can appreciate all options

3. MINDSET

Next is a word you have no doubt come across before, Mindset. This critical dimension of AQ-Ability, our Mindset, in our context correlates to our beliefs about change. Our perceived future experience in relation to changes is in part linked with optimism, hope, and our ability to visualise a positive future.

It's long been understood that our outlook and mindset have a disproportionate influence on the outcomes of our endeavours. At a basic level, if we believe in our ability to achieve something, we are infinitely more likely to achieve it.

As summarised in "The Direct and Indirect Effects of Employees' Mindsets on Job Performance" by Matt Zingoni & Christy M. Corey: "At one end of the continuum are those with an **entity mindset**; they believe that human attributes are fixed and cannot be changed. At the other end of the continuum are those with an **incremental mindset**; they believe that human attributes can be changed through effort and hard work. Where individuals fall on this continuum has been found to have profound effects on their thoughts and behaviours (e.g., Dweck, 1999; Dweck, Chiu, & Hong, 1995)."

Recent scientific research by Jason S. Moser, Carrie Heeter, Hans S. Schroder, and Yu-Hao Lee in *Psychological Science* has indicated "that neural mechanisms indexing on-line awareness of and attention to mistakes are intimately involved in growth-minded individuals' ability to rebound from mistakes".[13] In other words, people with a growth (incremental) mindset are more likely to detect errors than those without.

If we are to thrive in this ever-changing world, we have to embrace the incremental, growth mindset that not only can we change through effort, perseverance, and constant experimentation. But also that change is inert of positive or negative outcomes, it is the perception, context, and our beliefs which make such an association. An association, or prediction if you will, is influenced by our past experiences.

NEURAL FEEDBACK RESPONSE TO MISTAKES & PE AMPLITUDE

YOUR ERROR AWARENESS, & FUTURE PERFORMANCE, IS ASSOCIATED WITH YOUR MINDSET

FIXED MINDSET BRAINS

- NEURAL ACTIVITY CLOSES DOWN
- ERROR FEEDBACK TUNED OUT
- PROCESSING & CORRECTING SEEMS TOO DISTRESSING
- REDUCED FUTURE PERFORMANCE & ACCURACY

GROWTH MINDSET BRAINS

- HIGHTENED NEURAL ACTIVITY
- RAPID ERROR DETECTION
- ENHANCED ATTENTION TO CORRECTIVE FEEDBACK
- CONSCIOUS ATTENTION TO MISTAKES & IMPROVED FUTURE PERFORMANCE

Fixed Mind-Set   Growth Mind-Set

150–550 ms

0 µV   13.75 µV

THE PE DIFFERENCE AMPLITUDE FROM 150 TO 550 MS (AVERAGE ERP AMPLITUDE ON ERROR TRIALS – AVERAGE ERP AMPLITUDE ON CORRECT TRIALS) IN EACH OF THESE GROUPS.

SOURCE: JASON MOSER ET AL, 2011. MICHIGAN STATE UNIVERSITY, IDENTIFIED THE NEURAL MECHANISM TO EXPLAIN MINDSET IMPACT ON COPING & RESPONDING TO MISTAKES. "MIND YOUR ERRORS"

THE AQ GUY

LOW AQ MINDSET

"CHANGE IS NOT ALWAYS A GOOD THING"

→ Have a pessimistic outlook of the future

→ Believe change will result in bad outcomes

→ Negative when working towards goals

→ Hard to cope with change and challenges

→ Seek ways to avoid change

→ Negative view in the value of adapting

MEDIUM AQ MINDSET

"I'M UNSURE, BUT LET'S PROCEED CAREFULLY"

→ Have a balanced outlook

→ Adjusts to change when required

→ Occasionally uncertain about the future

→ Lack confidence with tough challenges

→ Can 'deal with' new situations

→ Can positively re-frame experiences

HIGH AQ MINDSET

"CHANGE ALWAYS LEADS TO GROWTH AND ABUNDANCE"

→ Strong optimistic outlook on the future

→ Believe they will thrive through change

→ Welcome new situations with positivity

→ **Have high levels of self-belief**

→ **Confidence in achieving goals**

→ **Adapt quickly to new situations**

4. RESILIENCE

The Oxford English Dictionary defines Resilience as: "the capacity to recover quickly from difficulties; toughness", or, in other words, the ability to "bounce back." Ledesma also defined resilience in near-identical terms: "the ability to bounce back from adversity, frustration, and misfortune" (2014). Our measure of resilience is based on 'The brief *resilience scale*' - BRS - which is the only measure that specifically assesses resilience in its original and most basic meaning: to bounce back or recover from stress (Agnes, 2005). This forms the basis of our assessment questions.

Resilience is one of the foundations of adaptability. As we have observed, adaptability is "the capacity to adjust one's thoughts and behaviours in order to effectively respond to uncertainty, new information, or changed circumstances." However, before we can "adjust" we have to process—on a psychological level—what this new information or environmental change means for us, and due to our inherent cognitive bias as a result of the evolutionary development of our brains, we tend to catastrophize. Therefore, before we can adequately and appropriately respond to these environmental or external stimuli, we have to cultivate a measure of *resilience*.

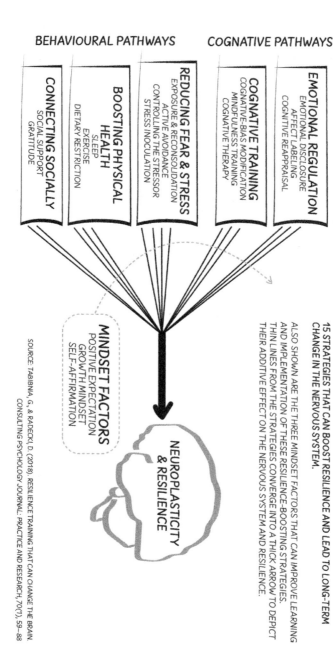

RESILIENCE TRAINING THAT CAN CHANGE THE BRAIN

BEHAVIOURAL PATHWAYS

COGNATIVE PATHWAYS

EMOTIONAL REGULATION
EMOTIONAL DISCLOSURE
AFFECT LABELING
COGNITIVE REAPPRAISAL

COGNATIVE TRAINING
COGNATIVE-BIAS MODIFICATION
MINDFULNESS TRAINING
COGNATIVE THERAPY

REDUCING FEAR & STRESS
EXPOSURE & RECONSOLIDATION
ACTIVE AVOIDANCE
CONTROLLING THE STRESSOR
STRESS INOCULATION

BOOSTING PHYSICAL HEALTH
SLEEP
EXERCISE
DIETARY RESTRICTION

CONNECTING SOCIALLY
SOCIAL SUPPORT
GRATITUDE

MINDSET FACTORS
POSITIVE EXPECTATION
GROWTH MINDSET
SELF-AFFIRMATION

NEUROPLASTICITY & RESILIENCE

15 STRATEGIES THAT CAN BOOST RESILIENCE AND LEAD TO LONG-TERM CHANGE IN THE NERVOUS SYSTEM.

ALSO SHOWN ARE THE THREE MINDSET FACTORS THAT CAN IMPROVE LEARNING AND IMPLEMENTATION OF THESE RESILIENCE-BOOSTING STRATEGIES. THIN LINES FROM THE STRATEGIES CONVERGE INTO A THICK ARROW TO DEPICT THEIR ADDITIVE EFFECT ON THE NERVOUS SYSTEM AND RESILIENCE.

THE AQ GUY

14

SOURCE: TABIBNIA, G., & RADECKI, D. (2018). RESILIENCE TRAINING THAT CAN CHANGE THE BRAIN. CONSULTING PSYCHOLOGY JOURNAL: PRACTICE AND RESEARCH, 70(1), 59–88.

Whilst we tend to think of resilience as something innate, almost like a trait of our personality, we can in fact learn to become more resilient. Psychologist Catherine Moore observed, "Resilience is something we can all develop, whether we want to grow as individuals, as a family, or as a society more broadly." It's a common idiom that negative experiences "build character" and studies have shown this to be the case.

The faster we are able to bounce back, the more resilient we are. Indeed, research shows that immediately following traumatic experiences, the brain actually becomes more neuroplastic.[15] Resilience theory even controversially argues that the nature of our adversity is largely irrelevant! What makes the difference is how we deal with it. This brings to mind the words of Mizuta Masahide, a seventeenth-century samurai and poet, "My barn having burned down, I can now see the moon."

Many of the greatest creators, innovators, and game-changers had incredible resilience. Thomas Edison, upon being accused of failing so many times to create the first electric light, said, "I have not failed. I've just found 10,000 ways that won't work."

Brené Brown, a research professor at the University of Houston and author of *Rising Strong*, expressed "Resilience is all about tolerance for discomfort". When we fail, rather than becoming overwhelmed, we simply try again.

As a reminder from the previous chapter on Grit, it is important to understand Grit is different to Resilience. Despite many people using the words interchangeably. Grit entails consistency of interests and goals over time, whereas the construct of resilience is "agnostic" on the stability of an individual's interests.

Through our research, we have identified the qualities of someone with high, medium or low resilience.

LOW RESILIENCE

"CHALLENGES SET ME BACK AND I TRY TO AVOID THEM"

→ Take a long time to recover from setbacks

→ Need support to recover from challenges

→ Seek stability

→ Reduced appetite for new things

→ Negative situations have a big impact

→ Higher risk of workplace stress

→

MEDIUM RESILIENCE

"GIVE ME TIME AND I WILL BE OKAY"

→ Can take longer to recover from setbacks

→ Stress increases with extreme challenges

→ Comfortable in 'coping & absorbing'

→ Confident with adapting incrementally

→ Anxious with transformative change

→ Comfortable with lower-risk

HIGH RESILIENCE

"SETBACKS, WHAT SETBACKS, I'VE MOVED ON ALREADY"

→ Recover quickly, with high endurance

→ Have a high capacity to bounce back and bounce forward

→ **Setbacks can be an energy stimulant**

→ **Challenges are an 'opportunity to grow'**

→ **Less affected by workplace stress, lower risk of burnout**

→ **Open to radical transformation**

5. UNLEARNING

The last ability element, but by no means least, is Unlearning, a two-fold dimension of adaptability, as it represents not only our passion and hunger for more knowledge but also our ability to let go of redundant information. As Barry O'Reilly observed in his book *Unlearn: Let Go of Past Success to Achieve Extraordinary Results*, "My inspiration to write *Unlearn* came from what I frequently find to be a significant inhibitor when helping high-performance individuals get better—not the ability to learn new things but the inability to unlearn mindsets, behaviours, and methods that were once effective but now limit their success." Success, or thriving, is as much about getting rid of what doesn't work as doing more of what does!

The process of unlearning is becoming especially critical in a world where the successful methodologies and approaches of yesterday are morphing into the very anchors and tethers holding us back. The trick is knowing when to let go of these past processes and strategies to make room for new ones that are more able to support our transformation into future success and growth.

Studies identify four key "influence levers" that help shift mindsets and therefore facilitate an unlearning process:

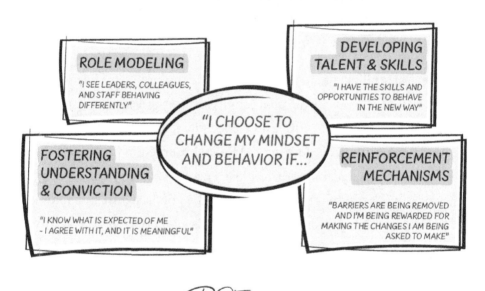

FOUR INFLUENCE LEVERS TO HELP SHIFT MINDSETS AND BEHAVIORS IN SUPPORT OF DESIRED CHANGE

ROLE MODELING
"I SEE LEADERS, COLLEAGUES, AND STAFF BEHAVING DIFFERENTLY"

DEVELOPING TALENT & SKILLS
"I HAVE THE SKILLS AND OPPORTUNITIES TO BEHAVE IN THE NEW WAY"

"I CHOOSE TO CHANGE MY MINDSET AND BEHAVIOR IF..."

FOSTERING UNDERSTANDING & CONVICTION
"I KNOW WHAT IS EXPECTED OF ME - I AGREE WITH IT, AND IT IS MEANINGFUL"

REINFORCEMENT MECHANISMS
"BARRIERS ARE BEING REMOVED AND I'M BEING REWARDED FOR MAKING THE CHANGES I AM BEING ASKED TO MAKE"

Ross Thornley THE **AQ** GUY

SOURCE: McKINSEY & COMPANY - THE FOUR BUILDING BLOCKS OF CHANGE

16

Role-modelling, fostering understanding, developing talent and skills, and reinforcement mechanisms. Collectively they form a very disciplined approach to leadership. However, because of inherent autonomy and freedom, leadership in agile organisations often comes from a self-disciplined approach—leading not in fear of punishment or sanction but in service of purpose and passion.

As Torben Rick observed in 2014: "Of the 500 companies that appeared on the first list [Fortune 500], in 1955, only 71 held a place on the list in 2008...

ORGANISATIONS, AND THE PEOPLE WITHIN THEM, MUST CONSTANTLY RE-INVENT THEMSELVES TO REMAIN COMPETITIVE."

This process of "re-invention" is the double-edged sword of letting go of the old and embracing the new. As Baron de Montesquieu observed when describing the 500-year success of the Roman Empire, "having fought successfully against all peoples, they always gave up their own practices as soon as they found better ones."[17]

As Barry O'Reilly puts it, "The Cycle of Unlearning isn't a one-and-done event. It's a system—a habitual, deliberate, and repeating practice of letting go and adapting to the situational reality of the present as we look to the future." Do check out his book titled *Unlearn* and our podcast interview together on Decoding AQ.

Unlearning is so important for breakthroughs and change—it is also a very effective area for delivering client value by facilitating and supporting people to commit to stop doing certain actions, no longer valuable in the new environment, *before* they do new things.

This learnable and improvable skill is an expanding topic, one where new research is emerging and expanding our understanding. Our unlearning is a valuable key to overcoming many of the biggest barriers and restrictions holding us back from transformative breakthroughs and rapid adaptation. It is important to distinguish unlearning from 'forgetting' or disregarding. It is a conscious choice to re-evaluate based on the new data and environmental factors. It is often an uncomfortable process, as we have a relationship with the past, how it made us feel, and the results we once experienced. It should be said not everything needs to be 'unlearnt' in order to break through.

Those with the highest levels of adaptability intelligence are situational and contextual beings; they are able to continually evaluate and tune into their own self-awareness to identify areas where they are struggling and feeling uncertain in their work or life. It might help to think of it like a product: we all experience products and software that get feature updates when new possibilities become available, in order to stay relevant in the market. It is the same for us. In order to stay relevant, we need to update our perceptions, knowledge, and behaviours on a regular basis.

LOW UNLEARNING

"IT WORKED BEFORE, SO IT WILL WORK AGAIN"

→ **Prefer to stick with known solutions**

→ **Protects current processes and solutions**

→ **Exhausted when problems seem unsolvable**

→ **Gains confidence from held knowledge**

→ **Described as 'stubborn' in your point of view**

→ **More prone to 'expert bias'**

MEDIUM UNLEARNING

"LET'S DISCUSS WHAT MIGHT WORK NOW"

→ **Able to explore new solutions to problems**

→ **Able to discuss a variety of perspectives**

→ **Able to let go of past patterns or behaviour**

→ **Feelings of uncertainty when 'letting go'**

→ Need more time and evidence to stop a course of action

→ Comfortable in changing course

HIGH UNLEARNING

"WE MUST CHANGE THE WAY WE DO IT, RIGHT NOW"

→ Find it easy to absorb new information

→ Can delete redundant data from brain

→ Able to let go of past patterns or behaviour

→ Embraces/champions multiple perspectives

→ Knows past wins do not guarantee future ones

→ Able to 'let-go' of existing processes easily

→ Break habits easily, champions change

AQ-CHARACTER

Our researchers have correlated key elements of personality to create a reliable framework for how our "personality", or rather the previously considered more fixed elements of Self, influences adaption. We specifically chose the word "Character" rather than "Personality" to distinguish our diagnostic, as we do not subscribe to the view that one's personality is fixed (more on this later). Though personality and Character are undoubtedly linked, we wanted to create a distinction: Character is something that may alter, or have different expressions, as a result of learning, contextual situations or a change of heart—for example, following a dramatic/traumatic experience—whereas historical models tend to see personality as static and fixed.

Though our learnable skills have perhaps the greatest impact on our adaptability, our Character also plays an important part and interacts with our adaptable skills in unique ways. If AQ-Ability is about how one adapts, AQ-Character is about understanding "**who**" is most likely to adapt and "**why**".

This is especially important when delivering feedback, either to clients, employees, or teams. We may have a sense of their overall adaptive abilities, which they can leverage and where they can improve. But if we do not understand their Character, we will not be able to speak to them effectively—to speak their language—in order to convey the message in a useful and sensitive way, and obtain the desired outcome or result we are seeking.

AQ-Character reveals underlying elements that might not be immediately obvious and could create conflict when challenged. For example, if someone has low Resilience, and we strategise with them about how they can increase their resilience by going to a group activity, not realising that they have an introversion preference, that is going to breed conflict, friction, and potential resentment barriers. Of course, that is an extremely obvious example, but it serves to illustrate the point that we must factor in a lot more than simply what appears on the surface. We must see the invisible.

In contrast to the AQ-Ability dimension, AQ-Character dimensions are measured on a preference scale, rather than a competence scale. This is because there is no "bad" profile (except, of course, the bad of not knowing!).

Building upon previous research into perhaps the most scientifically robust and valid personality measures, the Big Five, we have constructed our own unique model. It's important to note here that whilst these dimensions do show a correlation between certain "personality traits" and high adaptability, our current focus has been to build data within the specific context of work and change. You may achieve greater success and be highly adaptable in other areas of your life or indeed another role that is more aligned with your character.

The five sub-dimensions of AQ-Character are:

→ EMOTIONAL RANGE (THE EXTENT TO WHICH PEOPLE EXPERIENCE EMOTIONS BECAUSE OF SITUATIONS IN THEIR ENVIRONMENT).

→ EXTRAVERSION (HOW MUCH A PERSON SEEKS THE COMPANY OF OTHERS WHEN EXPERIENCING CHANGE).

→ HOPE (THE MINDSET TO PURSUE GOALS AND THE ABILITY TO SEE OR CREATE ALTERNATIVE WAYS TO REACH THEM IF CHALLENGED).

→ MOTIVATION STYLE (HOW EMPLOYEES MOTIVATE THEMSELVES AND WORK TOWARDS IMPORTANT GOALS, WHEN NAVIGATING CHANGE).

→ THINKING STYLE (HOW WE MAKE SENSE OF THE WORLD, HOW WE VIEW, CATEGORIZE & PROCESS INFORMATION IN OUR WORK ENVIRONMENT).

6. EMOTIONAL RANGE

Emotional Range relates to "neuroticism", or one's "predisposition to psychological stress". "High" neuroticism is typically seen as a predictor of depression, anxiety, and psychological disorder in general[18]. "Low" neuroticism correlates to a "stable" or "calm" personality type. Neuroticism measures our natural reactions and describes the extent to which people experience emotions because of situations in their environment.

In Part 1 of this book, we discussed how our amygdala has a tendency to hijack us and take control. The studies in neuroticism suggest that some people might indeed be more prone to this than others due to genetics. In fact, in 2015, scientists from Duke University discovered a specific gene variant linked to children who are "highly sensitive to their environments and are particularly vulnerable to stress. The genetic marker is part of the glucocorticoid receptor gene NR3C1 that influences the activity of a receptor to which cortisol binds and is directly involved in the stress response."[19] Children with the NR3C1 gene variant were proven to be more likely on average to develop "psychological problems" by age twenty-five (including substance abuse, aggression, and antisocial personality disorder) **if they did not receive the correct support**. This last part is absolutely vital. It wasn't that children with the NR3C1 gene—dubbed "orchid children" due to their heightened sensitivity—could not succeed, but having the correct environment was critical to their ability to flourish.

Much of the language used in studies into neuroticism from the '50s and '60s is highly negative and sociological. The subjective bias of the researchers has influenced our perception of neuroticism that it is entirely undesirable, whereas the example of "orchid children" shows that "far from being doomed, the children particularly sensitive to stress were also particularly responsive to help and had the capacity to become highly resilient, leading members of society".

Yes, we want to avoid being controlled by our amygdalas, in normal everyday situations, but on the other hand, the heightened awareness of those in a "neurotic" state can sometimes lead to spotting early warning signs that others miss.

Neuroticism or as we call it in our AQ model, **Emotional Range**, helps us to understand the level to which an individual worries, feels, and dwells on events. Whilst this may sound like a bad thing on the surface, we view it more in terms of being "reactive", and in fact, we observe in the natural world, in the behaviour of meerkats, that having "reactive" members of the population who are more alert to danger exponentially increases the survival odds of the colony. Neuroticism is not a disorder, but a continuum of experiences that all of us have throughout our lives. It is in part why we renamed this to emotional range in the context of adaptability, to move away from the past, negative bias.

This dimension is particularly relevant for situations of significant change, and times of increased uncertainty and therefore it has a very strong link to our adaptability intelligence.

As with all our character profile scores, this sub-dimension is scored on a sliding scale, **REACTIVE VS COLLECTED.** We might *need* to be highly reactive to create an adaption in a certain environment. If an organisation goes into crisis, one hopes that people will quickly rally to the cause and try to address the issues; sometimes, one can be too calm!

Our Emotional Range shows up based on the environmental stimulus. This means different stimuli or inputs will produce different outputs. We are measuring this in the context of the work environment, so people might be more reactive at home, or with their children, so remember this is looking at neuroticism in terms of work. It is important to consider that in our setting this is not about good or bad. It's about knowing when it's appropriate according to the situation, and what response suits which event best.

REACTIVE

"WHAT YOU SEE IS WHAT YOU GET"

→ Have higher stress responses

→ Suffer from more anxiety and worry

→ Have strong reactions to uncertainty

→ Overwhelmed at the unexpected

→ Lose your temper under high pressure

→ More sensitive when others are struggling

BALANCED

"I FEEL MANY EMOTIONS DURING CHANGE, BUT I AM MOSTLY IN CONTROL"

→ Experience both reactive and collective emotions as a result of

different situations

→ Have moments of worry and moments of calm and confidence. Context matters.

→ Be described as emotionally 'balanced'

→ Less likely to 'lose your temper' - Less triggered by extreme emotions resulting from different situations.

→ Act as an emotional facilitator, able to connect well with people experiencing change

COLLECTED

"I'M ALWAYS CALM UNDER PRESSURE,
WHATEVER LIFE THROWS AT ME, I'M NOT WORRIED"

→ Feel self-assured about the future

→ Calm when unexpected events happen

→ Control your emotions under pressure

→ Less worried and in control of reactions

→ Less sensitive with other people's struggles ·
Hardly ever dwells on negative events

7. EXTRAVERSION PREFERENCE

The first two dimensions of AQ-Character are both related to the Big Five. They represent the two Big Five traits identified as having the greatest correlation with adaptability. Whilst extraversion has a proven impact on AQ: "In meta-analyses, **EXTRAVERSION AND EMOTIONAL STABILITY HAVE OFTEN BEEN FOUND TO POSITIVELY PREDICT PERFORMANCE"**[20], This is not to say that those who are more introverted cannot be adaptable. As mentioned before, everything is contextual. Introverts can perform just as highly as extroverted individuals provided the environment, systems, and support are right (and the door swings both ways, as extroverts also need the right environment to perform). For example, an extravert working from home might find their energy significantly drained by isolation, whereas the introvert is able to harness this as a greater focus. Whilst we have to look at AQ-Ability, Character, and Environment separately for the sake of sanity, the reality is that the three are completely interrelated and ultimately viewing them holistically is the best practice. The value is in knowing the character to build hyper-personalised communications, interventions, and processes that unlock the flow of adaptability for each character preference.

We will not spend as much time unpacking Extraversion as we have some of the other sub-dimensions, as this topic has been covered extensively over the last fifty years in countless studies and research papers. However, it is important to understand that Extraversion has a direct influence on our interaction with technology, which is increasingly becoming an important factor in the modern world. "Gosling et al. (2011) showcased a positive relationship between extraversion and frequency of Facebook usage and engagement. Parallel to of-fline behaviour, extraverts seek out virtual social engagement, leaving behind a digital trail of behaviour such as friendship connections or picture postings"[21]. As our world becomes more technological, we can see that our AQ-Character may change with it in order for us to adapt to a more connected world.

Extraversion is a measure of our level of enthusiasm and energy, which plays an important role in decision-making. We are more likely to pursue goals, ex-periment, and try new things when we're in a highly excited mood. And if we don't get that high, we tend to fall back on safer choices.

Extraverted people are energised by social interaction, whereas introverted people are drained by it. Consider when you're at work whether you have lots of interactions with people, group presentations, and team meetings—do you feel energised afterwards, or do you feel drained and need to take a break, per-haps needing some alone time as you're exhausted? If the latter it's more likely that you may have a tendency to be more introverted as opposed to someone who seeks the company and stimulation of others.

Think of the world we live in right now...

Many people are now working remotely and will continue to do so long af-ter the pandemic. For some that might be energising, but for others, this isola-tion is a potential risk, this is very important for managers and leaders to know.

INTROVERTS DURING CHANGE

"I'VE GOT STUFF TO DO. I'M NOT 'MAD' I'M JUST THINKING"

→ Prefer stillness and time alone

→ Avoid loud, social work situations

→ Find intrusions distracting and disturbing

→ Like to keep your head down

→ Value 1-2-1 conversations about change

AMBIDEXTROUS DURING CHANGE

**"I ENJOY THE VARIETY; I LIKE BEING AROUND OTHERS,
    BUT I ALSO NEED TIME TO MYSELF"**

→ Gain energy and enthusiasm from different social situations

→ Enjoy change whether alone or in a team

→ Ambidextrous when dealing with change

→ Able to adapt to different social interactions, without negatively affecting your mood

→ Value a mix of 1-1 time alongside wider social group activities

EXTROVERTS DURING CHANGE

"MY TALKING, IS ME PROCESSING AND THINKING OUT LOUD"

→ Like to talk through change in groups

→ Gain energy from the company of others

→ Excited by attention and chatty environment

→ Suffers 'cabin fever' if isolated from others

→ Able to shift to new environments easily

8. HOPE

Hope is a very powerful word and one that has many associations with many people, particularly religious and spiritual associations. Most probably do not view this as a measurable personality or character trait but as a philosophical concept. Faith, Hope, and Love are said to be the three pillars of human morality, after all, according to St. Paul. However, there is a burgeoning academic interest in Hope as a measurable psychological state. Therefore, we wanted to expand upon this research in depth, as it may prove one of the vital keys to understanding AQ.

In essence, some people have a greater tendency toward hope (or optimism if you will).

We define hope as

"A POSITIVE MOTIVATIONAL STATE BASED ON AN INTERACTIVELY DERIVED SENSE OF SUCCESSFUL (A) AGENCY (GOAL-DIRECTED ENERGY) AND (B) PATHWAYS (PLANNING TO MEET GOALS)"[22].

We can draw out two key components from this: *agency*, which is the will-power or determination to pursue goals, and *pathways*, which is the "waypower" or ability to generate alternative paths and strategies to achieve goals when obstacles hinder plans. From our own data research, we see a correlation between Hope and Mental Flexibility and Unlearning. Hope is rooted in Snyder's extensive theory-building and research and has been applied to numerous life domains[23]. We further add the component of a goal, a vision for which we are hoping to attain.

The construct of hope is thus central to successful goal attainment[24] and goals are the engine for hope[25]. They provide the mental target to achieve. In addition, goals must be realistic and present at the right level of challenge to generate enough motivation[26]. Goals that are too difficult can lead to resignation or premature goal abandonment. Goals that are too easy, on the other hand, do not constitute a sufficient challenge to generate hopeful thinking.

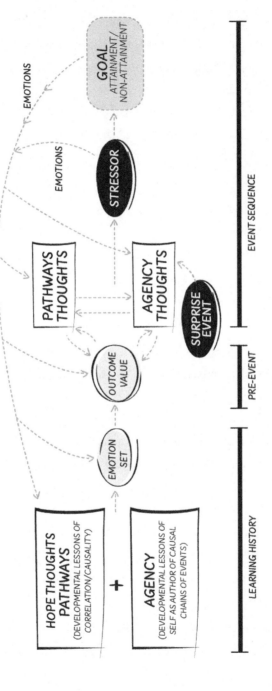

FEED-FORWARD & FEEDBACK FUNCTIONS INVOLVING AGENCY & PATHWAY GOAL-DIRECTED THOUGHTS IN HOPE THEORY

SOURCE: HOPE THEORY - SNYDER, 2000

THE AQ GUY

89

Hope has some resemblance with other positive psychology theories such as self-efficacy[27] and optimism theories[28]. Nevertheless, despite some similarities, only Snyder's hope model takes into account both agency and pathways components. Which gives greater indications of our adaptability when in pursuit of a goal. For instance, optimism, as well as self-efficacy theories, are mainly focused on **expectancies for success**, overlooking pathways thinking. In other words, hope also takes into account thoughts related to what individuals can do to achieve their goals.

In contrast, optimism is mainly focused on expectancies for future outcomes[29] which is a closer reflection of our AQ Mindset dimension. If we look at the self-efficacy theory, it focuses on beliefs about our capacities to achieve a desired goal. So, Snyder's theory of hope and Bandura's theory of self-efficacy are closest to the agency dimension of hope. Hope is one of the most powerful dimensions in our whole AQ model.

Initially, hope was conceptualised as a stable personality disposition. Consequently, a scale assessing hope at the dispositional level was developed and validated, Dispositional Hope Scale (DHS)[30]. Nevertheless, hope can also be represented as a temporary state related to particular events or specific moments (i.e. state level), which in the case of understanding adaptability behaviour was an important consideration in building our metrics. In order to assess hope situationally, the State Hope Scale was created and validated (SHS)[31]. Without identifying specific goals, the SHS measures a person's momentary hopeful thinking[32]. Back in the late '90s Snyder and colleagues showed the SHS and DHS were positively correlated, reflecting the fact that people with high dispositional hope generally report higher state hope levels.

Knowing how to measure the concept of Hope gave further opportunity to research the positive associations and outcomes in our work, lives, and society. The SHS has been positively associated with several variables such as state self-esteem, positive affect[33], self-efficacy[34], and negatively correlated with negative emotions[35] and burnout[36]. In addition, Irving and colleagues (2004) showed that state hope is associated with higher levels of well-being, fewer symptoms of depression, and increased coping abilities.

With respect to performance, state hope has been positively associated with performance in complex verbal learning tasks[37], anagram performance[38], academic achievement[39], and even track and field performances[40].

In a meta-analysis of 90 scientific studies on the effect of predictors of career adaptability, hope had the strongest effect among all predictors and was positively related to adaptability (rc = .69).[41] Additional research suggests the main reason why hope enables higher job proficiency is that it facilitates numerous advantageous cognitive processes. And my view is that these cognitive processes facilitated by hope are also likely to enable greater task adaptivity. Hopeful employees generate more strategies to achieve a goal and find more solutions when faced with novel and difficult problems[42], suggesting they will have more means with which to positively respond to change. Those with high levels of hope are more likely to interpret obstacles as challenges and persist in the face of setbacks[43], and to engage in problem-focused coping, further suggesting that they will be more adept at coping with change. In summary, hopeful employees are likely to find alternative ways to reach their goals as their working procedures change, they may identify alternative solutions when confronted with obstacles such as limited resources, and they are likely to approach changes in their core job as a challenge rather than a threat.

Whilst hope currently exists in our AQ-Character dimension, there is good news, the complexity of this *dispositional* and *state*-like trait gives rise to seeing this as a hybrid character trait, and a developable skill. Evidence shows it can indeed be developed through interventions[44]. Feldman and Dreher (2012) showed that hope can successfully be enhanced using a short 90-minute intervention[45] focused on "goal-pursuit". This was tested on the student population, and participants in the hope intervention showed "increases in measures of hope, life purpose, and vocational calling from pre- to post-test relative to control participants".

Supporting the idea that organisations might enhance constructive responses to change in their workforce by increasing levels of hope through training or mentoring[46], and through enhancing positive relationships with leaders[47].

FEARFUL/HOPELESSNESS

"I'LL MOST LIKELY FAIL. I DON'T KNOW HOW.
I'M NOT GOOD ENOUGH"

→ Low confidence and commitment in achieving goals

→ Fearful of new ways to achieve goals

→ Limited strategies to overcome challenges

→ Hard to identify ways to move forward

→ Lack of energy/emotion towards change

→ Resigned to disappointing outcomes

DOUBTFUL

"I'LL GET THERE WITH THE RIGHT HELP"

→ Have mixed feelings about the future

→ Be less confident which path to take

→ Need support when facing transformational change to overcome moments of fear and doubt

→ Unlock your potential through positive stories of
transformational change to enhance mindset

HOPEFUL

"THERE'S LIGHT AT THE END OF THE TUNNEL.
THINGS ALWAYS WORK OUT FOR THE BEST"

→ Believe in your ability to achieve your goals

→ Confident in overcoming challenges

→ High energy and like to move forward

→ Feel capable to overcome obstacles

→ Embrace uncertainty as opportunity

→ Value abstract thought and imagination

9. MOTIVATION STYLE

M otivation, alongside adaptability are increasingly becoming two
of the most important topics in the modern world.

WHAT DRIVES US?

WHAT KEEPS US MOTIVATED WHEN THE CHIPS ARE DOWN?

Our *Motivation Style* is one of the key aspects in understanding why we work
towards achieving our goals.

From an academic aspect Motivation or workstyle can be explained with
regulatory focus theory. The theory distinguishes between two systems of mo-

tivation that people use to achieve goals: a "promotion" focus concerned with maximising opportunities (we view this as a "burning ambition") and a "prevention" focus concerned with fulfilment of duties and minimising errors or mistakes (we view this as a "burning platform"—something you have to jump from!). Not only does it distinguish the motivation styles of employees when working towards goals but also explains the underlying emotional-cognitive mechanisms[48]. Promotion or prevention regulatory systems affect motivational needs, goal type, and orientation for gain or pain[49]. Recently scholars are also linking motivation styles to types of creativity, such as how radical new ideas are[50].

With a promotion focus, individuals are guided by aspirations and use what are known as "approach strategies" as they are motivated to accomplish gains. Individuals with a prevention focus are driven by safety and use avoidance behaviours as they are motivated to prevent negative outcomes.

Regulatory focus can explain work outcomes such as behaviours, high levels of performance, and other predictors (e.g. learning goal orientation or personality[51]). Regulatory focus theory also remains significant when controlling for other relevant individual factors such as affect[52] or chronic self-identity[53]. Moreover, both not only guide the strategic means to self-regulate towards the desired form of creativity[54], but also the two cognitive processes preceding creativity[55].

As a fundamental psychological driver, it describes not only why employees adapt to change, because of differences in what they desire, but how they adapt because of their unique strategies, behaviours and thoughts that result from their motivation style.

Motivation can be a tricky thing to understand. And it varies from person to person and importantly can even change depending on the situation. For a foundation level of understanding, there are two main types of motivation:

intrinsic and *extrinsic*. Intrinsic motivation is when you do something because it's enjoyable or fulfilling. Extrinsic motivation is when you do something to get something else. Generally speaking, intrinsic motivation is the more powerful of the two.

Our brains and bodies are designed to make us work towards goals. When our brains are motivated, the same areas that control rational thought and calculation are also stimulated. Intrinsic motivation is what makes us want to get to the end and achieve something. Extrinsic motivation can often be the reason we might take on tasks.

Don't confuse this dimension with what your **motivation is** e.g One might be motivated by money, mastery, recognition, control, connection, and such. What we are measuring in the AQme assessment is the 'style' of motivation in relation to a change. What triggers and drives you to make a given change?

My good friend, James Sale, perhaps the world's leading expert on motivation, correlates motivation to energy in his book *Mapping Motivation*, "Motivation is part of our future, and our ability to realise that future. No motivation means no energy."

In our model, we measure motivation in terms of preference on a continuum from

"PLAY TO PROTECT" to "PLAY TO WIN".

In other words, some people are motivated by protecting what they already have, a fear of loss, while others by a potential gain. Some of us adapt when we experience a **burning platform**, and others a **burning ambition.**

Let me share a quick example

The video conferencing software, Zoom, has been around a lot longer than the Covid-19 pandemic. A number of companies embraced it well before there was a need to, in part because they had a burning ambition to be better, they saw the gain, the advantages, not the loss of old and current communication methods. Whereas companies who have only embraced this technology as a result of the pandemic were forced to adopt to maintain workplace communication—they needed a burning platform.

To avoid confusion, let me iterate clearly: an individual on the "**play to protect**" end of the continuum is not more or less adaptable than a "**play to win**", they are simply motivated to adapt in different ways.

To dive deeper into the "play to protect" and "play to win" within the motivation style dimension, and their relation to our adaptive behaviours, let me summarise **Regulatory Focus Theory.**

REGULATORY FOCUS THEORY: SUMMARY

NEED	NURTURANCE (IN AQ LANGUAGE 'PLAY TO WIN')	SECURITY (IN AQ LANGUAGE 'PLAY TO PROTECT')
SELF-REGULATION OCCURS IN RELATION TO	IDEALS (E.G. HOPES, WISHES, & ASPIRATIONS)	OUGHTS (E.G. DUTIES, OBLIGATIONS, & RESPONSIBILITIES)
OVERARCHING GOAL	**ACCOMPLISHMENT** (GROWTH, ADVANCEMENT)	**SAFETY** (PROTECTION, SECURITY)
FOCUS OF SELF-REGULATION	**PROMOTION**	**PREVENTION**
SENSITIVITIES TOWARD	POSITIVE OUTCOMES	NEGATIVE OUTCOMES
SUCCESS (PLEASURE)	GAINS - BEHAVIOUR - APPROACH PLEASURE (I.E. PRESENCE OF POSITIVE OUTCOMES)	NON-LOSSES - BEHAVIOUR AVOID PAIN (I.E. ABSENCE OF NEGATIVE OUTCOMES)
FAILURE (PAIN)	NON-GAINS (I.E. ABSENCE OF POSITIVE OUTCOMES)	LOSSES (I.E. PRESENCE OF NEGATIVE OUTCOMES)
STRATEGIES[1] INSURE: INSURE AGAINST: PURSUIT CHARACTERIZED BY:[2]	HITS ERRORS OF OMISSION EAGERNES	CORRECT REJECTIONS ERRORS OF COMISSION VIGILANCE

 THE **AQ** GUY

SOURCE: IDSON, LIBERMAN, HIGGINS, 2000 (PP.252-254). 1. HIGGINS 1997 (P.1285). 2. HIGGINS 2000 (P.1219).

This sub-dimension insight provides helpful indicators for communication messaging within organisations. Knowing what will trigger adaptive behaviour for individuals and teams will remove friction, speed up change programs, and ultimately successful adaption outcomes.

On the next page, we can see how regulatory fit is achieved when working towards a goal.

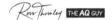

PLAY TO PROTECT

"WE CAN'T LOSE WHAT WE HAVE, IT IS TOO IMPORTANT"

→ Need a fear of failure in order to adapt

→ Ensure duties are fulfilled

→ Work carefully to assess the right solutions

→ Cautious and reliable in approach

→ Focus on avoiding negative outcomes

→ Adapt in an organised, tentative and sometimes slower way

CONTEXTUAL

"IT'S ALL ABOUT 'BALANCE' WE NEED TO FIND A WAY TO WIN, WITHOUT RISKING LOSING"

→ Can feel conflicted about which course to take

→ Seek to strike a balance between 'core' and 'new'

→ Feel like driving with one foot on the accelerator and one on the break at the same time

→ Can take longer to make decisions when the reason to change is unclear

→ When communication and plans are clear you can leap into action

PLAY TO WIN

"THE BIGGEST RISK IS NOT GOING BIG ENOUGH"

→ Need a burning ambition to adapt

→ Want to maximise gains

→ Take bigger chances to accomplish your aims

→ Energised by inspirational stories

→ Focus on achieving positive outcomes

→ Drive bold and higher risk actions

10. THINKING STYLE

The Thinking Style sub-dimension is related to how we **make sense of the world**, and how we view, categorise, and **process information** in our **work environment**. We all have a particular way of thinking. It's one of the most important things we can learn about ourselves.

As outlined in his 1997 book, *Thinking Styles,* Dr Robert J. Sternberg, an IBM professor of psychology and education at Yale University, shared his model and research on thinking styles, forms, and definitions. Including his theory of self-government. The theory of mental self-government is linked to the management of learners' own thinking styles, proposing thinking style is a preferred way of thinking, or a mode of thought, and is not regarded as "an ability", but as a way in which learners use their abilities (Sternberg 1990:366; 1994:36). The four core thinking style forms he outlines are; *The Monarchic, Hierarchic, Oligarchic,* and *Anarchic.* Broadly speaking the *monarchic* has a single-minded approach to problem-solving. Focus on one thing, set their mind to it, and pursue its completion without waiver. Often obsessive, the monarchic thinking style is so focused on the one *thing* they find it hard to deviate and change course. The *hierarchic* thinking style, on the other hand, forms a hierarchy of goals and understands the need to set priorities, as they believe not all goals can be achieved (or at least not fulfilled equally well). As a result, this style tends to deal with and accept complexity and change to a greater degree than the *monarchic style.* This style makes for good facilitators and project managers. It is aligned in part to a central reading in the AQme profile: able to consider their thinking style preference in relation to context, competing demands, and prioritisation. The oligarchic thinking style is most similar to the hierarchic, in having the desire to do more than one thing within the same time frame. However, individuals with this style of thinking perceive competing goals as of equal importance, regularly feeling pressure to achieve all goals within the same time and with the same resources, not confident in which to pursue or follow first, and how much time to give to each. This thinking style can be harnessed with simple guidance and support as to the prioritisation of the organisation or team. And finally *anarchic* appears to be haphazard in their approach, perhaps randomly jumping from one goal to another, which can create confusion and be difficult for others to understand. Anarchic thinking styles often reject rigid systems, and cause conflict when they feel constrained by processes. Elements of this theory of thinking style have been incorporated into our mental flexibility skill, the ability to explore information gathered from multiple sources and creatively combine to ideate new solutions.

This theory of thinking styles has valuable inputs. However, it focuses more on how people apply action to problem-solving, and less on why they might adapt. Hence why aspects have been considered in the AQ-Abilities dimension. In our model of AQ-Character, we have included some principle concept elements from self-government, combined with that of "learning and chunk size" outlined in Dr Fiona Beddoes-Jones' 1988 book, *Thinking Styles Relationship Strategies that Work,* relating to the natural preference for the size of the information required. The bigger the preference for chunk size, the less information will be required. A continuum from detailed, conscious thinking, to big-picture, strategic thinking.

Through our research we have discovered as people go through their careers they often become **ambidextrous** in their styles of thinking in order to progress and **level up**. We might build the capability of both **big picture** and **detailed thinking** as we become more capable through experience and time. When **teams become highly successful they leverage these two different aspects** to navigate through situations of change and opportunity. Some individuals and the best companies have this poetic dance between 'zoom-out' and 'zoom-in' strategy. In our AQme assessment, we are looking to identify the **strongest style preference in the context of change**.

Our thinking style can also **change depending on the situation and the environment**. I was involved in launching a version of the Hartman Value Inventory in 2008 in the UK, developed from the work of Robert Schirokauer Hartman, a German-American logician and philosopher. His primary field of study was scientific axiology and he is known as its original theorist. His axiology is the basis of the Hartman Value Inventory, which found that when we are under high pressure and stress our deepest and sometimes hidden values show up. There is an important link to understand: one might be a very collaborative and a big picture thinker in most day-to-day situations, however, when under high stress, when required to adapt rapidly, we might shift to the details and narrow our focus.

Therefore it is important to identify **when change happens**—when we **need to radically adapt**—do we focus on the big picture or the details? Remember it is not about capability in either, in fact, you might balance both, but what we measure is your **natural instincts at the point** of adaptation and change.

One of the merits of understanding Thinking Style in your adaptability profile expands the potential for the task and environmental *fit*. Society has long judged people with potentially equal abilities differently, due to the nature of those individuals whose styles better match the certain situation and the tasks they are facing. If we are able to adapt and modify the tasks or the given style to align with the specific task or change required we are better able to unlock higher performance and levels of positive emotional health. It is in the mind of the beholder as to the perception of fit—dead-end job, or dream job—when the work is a misfit to the way in which one thinks and uses the talents and skills they have.

Those with a preference toward a broad and big-picture thinking style focus on the primary outcome of a given goal, often trying to connect the dots between their various roles and responsibilities at work to create an overarching job definition. When interacting with others, their thinking style may be especially useful in ensuring their peers remember the end goal, great to "keep people on track", yet they are also more likely to give ambiguous instructions or overstep boundaries in their attempt to address broad objectives. In short, they will see the forest but at times overlook the trees.

Now, a person with a specific and detailed thinking style generally makes sense of their work by seeing the (often hidden) details in the picture. Their thinking style at work is rather specific, detailed, and focused on concrete processes or steps toward achieving a goal. Individuals with this thinking style also try to separate the various roles and responsibilities they have and address each with the required input at hand. When interacting with others, their thinking style may be especially good to ensure their peers are aware of the necessary steps they must take to achieve a goal—yet they are also more likely to get lost in details if in management they can sometimes be perceived as 'micromanaging'.

DETAILS

"WE MUST HAVE A PLAN FOR THIS TO BE SUCCESSFUL"

→ **See hidden details**

→ **Be very specific and concrete in process**

→ **Like to separate roles and responsibilities**

→ **Establish steps required for achieving goals**

→ Can be perceived as micromanaging

→ Can get lost in the minutiae

CONNECTOR

"PEOPLE KNOW I GET THINGS DONE AROUND HERE"

→ Make great project facilitators

→ One eye on the prize the other on planning the steps and process to achieve it

→ Less likely to initiate and push the boundaries of thinking at the macro (very large) and micro (minuscule) levels

→ Connect with others at both ends of this range

→ Rarely the ones who envisage a transformative future or solution

BIG PICTURE

"YOU'RE MISSING THE POINT... THIS IS WHY WE ARE DOING IT"

→ Be all about the primary outcome

→ Joins dots between roles and responsibility

→ Keep people on track

→ Give ambiguous instructions

→ Push boundaries in pursuit of objectives

→ See the forest, but overlook the trees

AQ-ENVIRONMENT

O ur environment can boost or inhibit our adaptability. In the example of the orchid children, "when the children with the NR3C1 gene variant participated in intensive support services, only 18% developed problems as adults", as opposed to 75% if left "untreated"[56]!

We must remember that our environment is not merely a physical space we inhabit, but an interconnected network of factors ranging from interpersonal ones, such as Emotional Health, Team Support, and Company Support, to managerial / organisational factors, such as Work Stress or Work Environment. In the case of the orchid children, support services are highly correlated with AQ-Environment sub-dimensions such as Team Support. By changing the environment and providing the necessary support—a team that could nurture the children in the right ways—the children were able to thrive and achieve their full potential.

But how can we recognise whether an environment is helping or hindering our adaptability? Here is a handy quick-reference table.

HOW TO SPOT ENVIRONMENTS WHICH SUPPORT HIGHLY ADAPTABLE BEHAVIOURS

LOW ADAPTATION ENVIRONMENT	**HIGH** ADAPTATION ENVIRONMENT
• FEEL ISOLATED	• FEEL VALUED
• REGULARLY EXPERIENCE NEGATIVE EMOTIONS	• REGULARLY EXPERIENCE JOY & EXCITMENT
• SHARING NEW IDEAS IS RISKY	• SHARING NEW IDEAS IS CELEBRATED & REWARDED
• AVOID PROBLEMS	• BRING UP ISSUES WITHOUT JUDGEMENT
• HIDE MISTAKES	• OPENLY DISCUSS MISTAKES ACROSS WHOLE ORGANIZATION
• UNABLE TO FINISH TASKS	• ABLE TO FINISH TASKS

Ross Thornley THE **AQ** GUY

AQ-Environment asks the question "**When** does someone adapt and to what degree?" This is all about the critical importance of context. Gregory Bateson (creator of the double-blind theory of schizophrenia) theorised that "man's only real self is the total cybernetic network of man plus society plus environment."[57]

Rarely if ever is the environment or context ever taken into account in psychometrics or self-perception inventories. I believe this is one of the greatest oversights in the people data and assessments industry. This can be a deciding factor in our overall capacity to thrive and navigate change. You might have all the adaptability skills in the world, but if you feel unsupported, judged, highly stressed, and unsafe, chances to use those skills in anything but survival situations will be severely limited.

This is demonstrated in a 2018 white paper study on the future of the workforce by The Adecco Group & The Boston Consulting Group which revealed a disconnect: "between employees' willingness to acquire new skills (some 62% of employees consider themselves as primarily responsible for acquiring these) and the degree to which they will take the initiative (59% expect their employer to develop the training opportunities).

WORKERS SEE THE MAIN OBSTACLES TO ACQUIRING NEW SKILLS AS THE LACK OF TIME AND THE COST OF TRAINING."

Studies have shown one of the four factors that facilitate learning is "developing talent and skills", yet here we see that environmental factors—aka the "lack of time" and "cost of training"—prevented employees from developing new skills, which in turn had a knock-on effect on the development of the business. Again, to understand this more fully we have to remember AQ-Environment is far more holistic than simply a place we work. Lack of time may not appear to be an environmental factor, but it is, because employees are not in control of the amount of work they are allocated—this is decided by upper management. Indeed, we measure the sub-dimension of Work Stress in terms of "overwhelm"—whether someone feels capable of managing their workload. This directly correlates with the time employees have to complete additional tasks, such as training—an employee with high Work Stress is unlikely to have any spare time or indeed brain-space to attend to developmental exercises. Additionally, the cost of training is another environmental factor because it relates to Company Support—to what extent the organisation is prepared to invest in its people, whether that investment is financial or otherwise (not all investments are of money, after all).

Following significant research we built our AQ Environment dimension with the following five sub-dimensions:

→ COMPANY SUPPORT (THE GENERAL PERCEPTION EMPLOYEES HAVE AROUND THE EXTENT TO WHICH THEIR ORGANISATION VALUES THEIR CONTRIBUTIONS AND CARES ABOUT THEIR WELLBEING).

→ EMOTIONAL HEALTH (THE DEGREE IN WHICH INDIVIDUALS ARE THRIVING AT WORK, BY EXPERIENCING POSITIVE MOMENTS WHILE LIMITING THE NEGATIVE ONES).

→ TEAM SUPPORT (THE EXTENT TO WHICH EMPLOYEES FEEL THEY CAN SHARE KNOWLEDGE, ARE SUPPORTED THROUGH CHALLENGES, AND FEEL THEY CAN OPENLY DISCUSS THEIR OPINION).

→ WORK ENVIRONMENT (DOES YOUR ORGANISATION FACILITATE AND ENCOURAGE SELF DISRUPTION, RAPID EXPERIMENTATION, AND REGULAR ADAPTION, OR DOES IT HAMPER THEM)?

→ WORK STRESS (THE SENSE OF GENERAL OVERWORK AND OVERWHELM WITHIN YOUR ORGANISATION).

The Research and Science Basis of AQ-Environment

The links between environment and adaptability have been established through studies and research. Research[58] linking "perceived management support" with "employee readiness for change" defined "readiness for change" as **"the extent to which members of an organisation regard a change positively and anticipate that it will be a good thing for themselves and their organization."** This is an important definition, as we see increasingly that organisations want their staff to be "change ready" but don't know how to go about creating the correct environment to foster this state.

Furthermore, research has shown: "On a day-to-day basis, support from management helps **employees cope with the demands of their role** (Bakker, Demerouti, & Verbeke, 2004), with **clear positive effects for organisational outcomes** such as employee **engagement, motivation** and **well-being**[59]. **These effects persist in the context of organisational change, such that supportive relationships lead to more positive employee attitudes toward change**[60], which in turn help employees to proceed effectively with the tasks of change61. I commonly hear people refer to a "support network", but this is exactly what most people need, whether this is a technological support network, or a human, social one. We cannot adapt to our fullest extent if we do not have the correct support in place from management, colleagues, and even friends.

This also relates to **leadership**, which is why our assessment tool also provides deeper insights specifically for coaches and management.

There is growing interest in issues of authenticity in organizational life[62] focused on individuals behaving in ways that reflect inner and self-transcendent values[63]. For example, authentic leaders manage values such as honesty, loyalty, and equality in their interactions with followers to gain relational authenticity[64]. From this perspective, leaders draw from personality resources to foster self-awareness and self-regulated positive behaviours toward their followers.[65]

However, AQ Environment is also about a wider landscape, and more recently the increasing impact of technology.

Research published in 2018 suggests, that in the United States, a 10% increase in the likelihood of being affected by automation is associated with decreases in the physical and mental health of 0.8% and 0.6%, respectively.

IN OTHER WORDS, THERE IS A DIRECTLY OBSERVABLE CORRELATION BETWEEN THE PERCEPTION OF CHANGE IN OUR ENVIRONMENT AND OUR MENTAL WELL-BEING.

Wider changes in the structure of work and in its place in society are further sources of potential stress. Job security and stability are in decline in many advanced economies, with earnings growth sluggish or stagnating and less predictable "gig economy" and flexible work expanding.

Evidence from the workplace reinforces concerns about growing problems with mental health. In the United Kingdom, an independent review found that while sickness-related absences overall fell by more than 15% between 2009 and 2017, absences related to mental health problems increased by 5%.

We need only look to the Covid-19 pandemic and the effects of lockdown to observe how environmental changes can drastically alter our mental health, with stress levels now at an all-time high. In fact, the UK Government's "COVID-19 mental health and wellbeing surveillance: report": "suggests the proportion of adults aged 18 and over reporting a clinically significant level of psychological distress increased from 20.8% in 2019 to 29.5% in April 2020." And more contemporary research from February 2022 shows, "Overall, people with existing psychiatric disorders are experiencing a detrimental impact on their mental health from the COVID-19 pandemic, for example in OCD and PTSD, which requires close monitoring in clinical practice... Longitudinal observations with an adequate time of follow-up suggest an increased risk for suicidality associated with the pandemic... Regarding children and adolescents diagnosed with a psychiatric disorder, studies have generally reported a worsening of symptoms in young patients with eating disorders, obsessive-compulsive disorders, and neurodevelopmental disorders such as ADHD and ASD. Severe mental illness in turn has been shown to represent an important vulnerability factor for COVID-19 infection"[66]

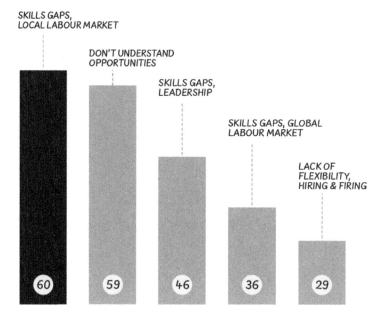

BARRIERS TO TECHNOLOGY ADOPTION BY US COMPANIES WITHIN THE NEXT 4 YEARS

A SURVEY OF 313 COMPANIES, REPRESENTING OVER 15 MILLION EMPLOYEES
(% SHARE OF COMPANIES SURVEYED)

SKILLS GAPS, LOCAL LABOUR MARKET — 60

DON'T UNDERSTAND OPPORTUNITIES — 59

SKILLS GAPS, LEADERSHIP — 46

SKILLS GAPS, GLOBAL LABOUR MARKET — 36

LACK OF FLEXIBILITY, HIRING & FIRING — 29

SOURCE: DATA FROM THE WORLD ECONOMIC FORUM - FUTURE OF JOBS SURVEY 2018

Previously studies, like the one pictured above, showed the biggest barrier for technology adoption in the last decade was considered to be skills-related, followed by lack of understanding of the potential opportunities (correlated to Mindset). However, this is very much old news, and things have shifted dramatically in terms of perception and culture. A new survey we conducted on over 500 business coaches and consults revealed that the biggest barrier to change was no longer anything to do with skills. In fact, the skills gap was only considered a barrier to change in 1.8% of respondents. The greatest obstacle now, according to those in the field, is **leadership**, and by quite some margin.

THE BIGGEST OBSTACLES BUSINESSES FACE WHEN ADAPTING TO CHANGE

A SURVEY OF 529 BUSINESS COACHES & CONSULTANTS, BASED IN USA, UK AND EUROPE.

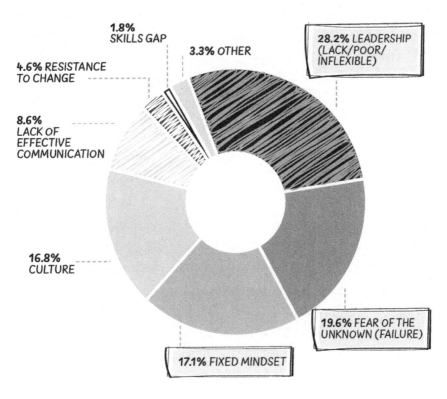

1.8% SKILLS GAP

3.3% OTHER

4.6% RESISTANCE TO CHANGE

8.6% LACK OF EFFECTIVE COMMUNICATION

28.2% LEADERSHIP (LACK/POOR/INFLEXIBLE)

16.8% CULTURE

19.6% FEAR OF THE UNKNOWN (FAILURE)

17.1% FIXED MINDSET

SOURCE: AQai RESEARCH REPORT 5 BIGGEST OBSTACLES BUSINESSES FACE WHEN ADAPTING TO CHANGE - 2022.

 THE **AQ** GUY

AQai.

This reflects a tremendous thinking shift, in my mind. To say that the barrier to change is skills-gap related reinforces a traditional "top-down" approach to leadership. The employee, in other words, is at fault for not having the skills equal to the task at hand. Therefore, we either need to train them or bin them. However, to perceive inadequate leadership as a barrier to change is very much a bottom-up approach to matters, for it suggests that the responsibility for navigating change is not with the employee (though of course, we all play our part) but with the top management. I also think this is very wise: we need to change at the top level, to role-model what change looks like *before* we can change at any other level. Asking our employees to shift their skills and thinking before we have shifted them ourselves is likely to lead to problems. Clearly, these studies reveal a culture caught in the liminal space—a transformational shift—between these two polarities. What a time to be alive!

Our adaptability skills interrelate with our Environment in powerful ways, and leaders are responsible for curating environments. Where there is poor or lacking leadership, there is no environmental safety, and no vision of the future to work towards. It's no surprise people feel that lack of or poor leadership is a major barrier to change. After all, we look to leaders to show the way! However, is it the case that the world lacks good leaders, or that leaders themselves are struggling and do not have the right resources and tools to empower them to lead? We at AQai firmly believe that we are navigating the most significant period of change in human history. Humanity is being put to the test like never before; this is a whole new landscape. And so, we need new tools to combat this seemingly scary new environment, tools that will help us learn there is actually a wealth of opportunity once we get beyond the fear response.

Just as studies have shown our Environment can negatively impact our ability to adapt and negatively impact our mental-wellbeing, the reverse is also true. Our lack of adaptability skills can fail to allow us to take advantage of our Environmental opportunities.

11. COMPANY SUPPORT

The general perception employees have around the extent to which their organisation values their contributions and cares about their wellbeing. We often see high levels of company support correlated to job performance, satisfaction, and lower staff turnover. If employees see their company as generally supportive and caring, they are more likely to adapt to any required changes and even attempt to align their goals with company ones.

In challenging times, when leaders in an organisation are under pressure, it is rare that a company will put employees before the goals and concerns of the company. The different approaches made in the aviation industry by two different airports, when global travel came to standstill, provide an indication of company support in action. In the UK, like many countries, there were wide and vast layoffs. Check-in and boarding gates became ghost towns, as the term furlough became part of our common language. This was an act of survival, with an unknown future, and no clear dates to predict when government restrictions against travel would be lifted. International travel was grounded. The ability of airports and airlines to effectively plan capacity, demand, and resources was so difficult, so unknown, that the liminal space created fear and tremendous anxiety. For how long could they 'hang on'? Could the numerous grants and subsidies help the industry hold until the skies would once again be open?

Let me share a story about the different strategies between the second busiest airport in the UK—Gatwick —and Italy's second busiest Milan Malpensa. It paints an interesting picture of the complexity of company support strategies.

Gatwick airport officially opened on the 9th of June 1958, reaching passenger numbers of over 46 million in 2019. Almost half of those travelling with the airline, EasyJet. However, in 2020 Gatwick lost some 78% of its passenger traffic, falling to 10 million, and 40% further still to 6 million in 2021[67]. Gatwick is privately owned and operated by VINCI Airports, boasting the world's largest and most diversified network, with 46 airports in 12 countries. Bringing together about 18,500 employees worldwide, including the 3,200 employees in London Gatwick. It was reported in October 2021 that the airport was paying staff to "stay at home", losing some £1m per day. More than half of the airport's 1,787 staff were not needed because it was operating at a heavily reduced capacity. It had already lost 46% of its staff since the start of the pandemic. With rising concerns about letting more staff go, they resorted to paying full wages to the remaining employees who were not working for chunks of the week, so they would be ready to return when demand for travel rebounded. They would be asked to clock some of the hours as unpaid overtime if capacity returned to normal in 2022. This would see some staff "working back" up to one extra shift each month in the summer, according to HR director David Conway at the time.

This challenge was not a lone story: thousands of workers in the airline industry around the world were axed as the pandemic grip took hold. Aviation lost 2.3 million jobs globally during the pandemic, with ground-handling and security hardest hit[68]. Gatwick Airport staff received millions of pounds of support from the Government's furlough scheme before it ended in September 2021. The business claimed £39.6m between April 2020 and June 2021 to temporarily lay off around 53% of its staff.

Whilst this strategy appears like an attempt to put staff first, making substantial losses in the process, I can't help but think this was only really meeting the basic financial needs of the half who remained employed. Many companies leveraged the furlough scheme here in the UK to help fund the salaries of employees who were not able to work. However, in my view, this created a disconnect from each other, and importantly the company. For Gatwick staff, being asked to "stay home", they were no longer able to interact with each other, lost the sense of belonging and purpose; they were abandoned on the arid plains of a desert. Many sought alternative futures, shifting from their roles in security and baggage handling to more flexible work, lured by the gig economy or opting to retire early. What a loss from the lack of leveraging all the potential creative innovations and intellectual capital by not redeploying and re-imagining how people might contribute.

Across Europe, airports such as Brussels, Frankfurt, and Amsterdam experienced some of the chaos we've seen here in the UK. But not all countries reacted to Covid-19 in the same way.

Milan Malpensa, the second busiest airport in Italy, was first opened in 1909 by Giovanni Agusta and Gianni Caproni to test their aircraft prototypes. It switched to civil operation in 1948. With over 28 million annual passengers in 2019, much like every other airport, passenger numbers fell to 7 million in 2020, down 72%. What is starkly different is not a single one of their 2,788 staff[69] lost their job due to Covid-19!

Italy was one of the first parts of the Western world to be hit by the pandemic, and the government took the decision to step in with an extensive and expensive financial aid package, including extended furlough and an 800 million euro cash subsidy. This very strong and robust scheme came with some small print: it forbade any layoffs. So unlike many airports now scrambling to fill roles, unable to recruit talent, despite multiple incentives, for Milan, everybody just came back to work.

What is also important is the airport used the extra money to invest in new technology. Engaging the workers to discover and innovate ways to improve their and the passengers' experience. This led to multiple initiatives including deploying some of the cash subsidy funds to upgrade the security machines to the latest generation with two key features. One is that they enable 30% more throughput. With the new machine, same staff, 30% more luggage through. The second feature greatly improves the passenger experience because you don't need to take liquids and computers out of your bag, it can scan them directly inside. This removes friction for passengers and is a far better experience for the staff too. Just think: no more little clear bags of liquids, or struggling to get your iPad and laptop out. The workers felt involved, and connected, and did not look for alternative fulfilment and new roles. Now the airport is able to run more efficiently and the only chaos felt by passengers is the knock-on effects from other airports failing to function and causing delays and cancellations.

The effects of the decisions made in the waves of the pandemic have created a stark and discontented reality as people return to adventure once again on international travel. Major staff shortages, strikes, thousands of flight cancellations, and eye-watering long queues at major airports around the world. The level of last-minute flight cancellations from the UK was up 188% in June 2022, compared to June 2019[70]. After sweeping job cuts and pay cuts when COVID-19 brought travel to a grinding halt, staff across the industry from pilots to baggage handlers are now asking for big pay increases and better working conditions. There are currently 2,884 jobs unfilled in UK airports (280 of those at Gatwick) with airlines also recruiting to fill a further 660 roles[71]. Demand for cleaners has surged by 731% year-on-year with security officer vacancies rising by 200%[72].

The sub-dimension of company support seeks to measure to what extent the company not only cares about employee wellbeing, and puts its workforce before its own goals and concerns, but most importantly reveals whether employees believe there is genuine concern and a willingness to help in times of need.

LOW COMPANY SUPPORT

"I'M JUST A NUMBER, MAYBE I DON'T BELONG HERE"

→ See employer as distant and uncaring

→ Feel isolated, and question belonging

→ Believe employer lacks interest in you

→ Concerned about lack of support

→ Feel employer doesn't value wellbeing

→ Become disengaged, and less committed

MEDIUM COMPANY SUPPORT

"I DON'T FEEL A REAL CONNECTION OR SPARK HERE"

→ Believe employer shows some interest

→ Perceive support sometimes as 'box-ticking'

→ Unsure if contributions matter to employer

→ Apathetic towards new employer initiatives

→ Have varying levels of engagement

→ Question if employer cares about wellbeing

HIGH COMPANY SUPPORT

"I KNOW MY COMPANY CARES ABOUT ME AND HAS MY BACK"

→ Have high loyalty and engagement

→ Experience employer caring about you

→ Feel highly valued and in greater alignment

→ **Go further, even if it might be hard**

→ **Feel very supported and take on more proactive responsibility**

→ **Be less likely to leave**

12. EMOTIONAL HEALTH

E motional Health in our context of adaptability refers specifically to the degree to which individuals are **thriving** at work, **experiencing positive emotions and moments while limiting the negative ones.** The emotional health we measure focuses on the energy to engage in continuous change and adapt in times of the unknown. With an increase in positive experiences around change at work, companies can build a good foundation for long-term change. There is mounting research about the negative effects of our emotional health not only on our work performance and ability to have a successful relationship with change, but on the lasting impacts of sustained periods of anxiety, worry, and nervousness about the unknown.

Thriving is defined as the psychological state in which individuals experience both a sense of **vitality** and learning[73]. This sense of vitality and learning is core to our model of adaptability. The research by Porath et. al established a relationship between thriving and career development initiative, burnout, health, and individual job performance, explaining significant variance beyond traditional attitudinal predictors, such as job satisfaction and organisational commitment. They also focused on understanding the contextual embeddedness of thriving. Discovering differences in reports of thriving across two points in time, when substantial changes are occurring in peoples' work lives and across contexts (i.e., work and non-work).

Understanding Emotional Health is an essential data point to gather around the vitality and emotional state you and your employees are facing whilst at work in order to understand its impact on individual and organisational adaptability.

Those who score low on our Emotional Health scale are at risk of failing to adapt to changes as they experience negative emotions more frequently at work. They would typically report these negative experiences as sadness and anxiety in the workplace. At the same time, their positive experiences are limited, and they rarely feel excited or relaxed. In the long term, this is likely to lead to high employee turnover, burnout, or general apathy as employees have extended periods of "giving up trying" to adapt within the organisation.

People with medium reported levels of Emotional Health may appear to be stuck in a state of inertia when it comes to positive or negative experiences in the workplace. In our own research individuals report feeling like they don't know whether they are coming or going. They experience periods of sadness and anxiety, and might even show early signs of apathy. This state and environment are not conducive to a productive and highly adaptable situation. Whilst they have elements of positive experiences there is a danger that these are too often overshadowed by negative ones.

Conversely, those who score highly within our Emotional Health scale are **thriving** at their company and thus are better positioned to have a high adaption capacity. They report only limited negative experiences. Positive experiences at work, such as excitement or relaxation, are the norm rather than the exception. This provides a solid foundation for long-term, and continual change as these people have the energy and the emotionally positive environment to adapt well in their organisation, even if the change required is perceived to be difficult.

Thriving employees performed 16% better, were 125% less likely to feel burnout, and were 32% more committed to their organisation[74].

When organisations fail to enable a sense of thriving in their workforce, there are several consequences. As reported by Mercer in their white paper, "Thriving in an age of disruption": "First, organisations fail to adapt effectively to the changes in their external environment. They miss emerging technology trends, fall behind on anticipating their customer's wants, and fail to capitalize on growth opportunities." Secondly, innovation is stifled, with employee relationships shifting to more transactional operations; staff feel less invested in. And finally, decision-making processes are led more by drama than data, as the organisation is unable to harness information about their business and workforce to make the right decisions.

LOW EMOTIONAL HEALTH

"CHANGE IS MORE OFTEN BAD, AND I DON'T LIKE IT"

→ Regularly experience negative emotions

→ Have a low adaption capacity and feel unable to adapt to current changes

→ 'Bogged down' and nervous about change

→ Felt sadness/anxiety in the workplace

→ Find your workplace a stressful place to be

→ Benefit from support & Environmental change

MEDIUM EMOTIONAL HEALTH

"I'M NOT BOTHERED EITHER WAY"

→ Feel stuck, unsure coming or going

→ Signs of calmness, can be seen as apathy

→ Be less likely to drive change

→ Negative emotions overshadow positive ones

→ Experience moments of anxiety and sadness

→ Sense short-lived flashes of positivity

HIGH EMOTIONAL HEALTH

"I CAN'T WAIT FOR THE NEXT PROJECT AND EXPERIENCE"

→ Sense of thriving, workplace champion

→ High tolerance and capacity for adaption

→ Experience joy, excitement & contentedness

→ Can sustain positivity during change

→ Rarely experience negativity at work

→ Reassured that the environment supports your mental health

13. TEAM SUPPORT

Within the AQ model, *Team Support* refers directly to the team environment in which employees feel they can share new knowledge, are supported through challenges and feel they can openly discuss their opinion. Employees who work in supportive teams are more likely to try new ways to adapt in times of change and can build on team support to sustain adaptive behaviour over time. Think of it as the collective emotional readiness of a group to be themselves, which leads to highly adaptive team members.

Team support is a key component of psychological safety—a powerful tool for building trust, connection and support within a team. And a key component to the right environment for a highly adaptable and successful workforce. For leaders, psychological safety is one of the most important assets. The ability to create a safe space among their team members is vital to success. This type of environment allows people to communicate openly and express themselves without fear of attack or criticism. It is the opposite of being afraid to speak up or share your ideas, and it's a necessary prerequisite to a healthy team. Both the good news and the challenge is that the environmental results are based on an individual's current perceptions of where they are, today. So if they change teams, or change their environment, it is likely to change their result, so this is very dynamic. If an individual changes teams, I recommend they retake the AQme assessment 3 to 6 months after the shift in order to see how their percep-tions of team support have changed.

This dimension can also be an early-warning barometer as to the reality of diversity and inclusion behaviours. Taking inputs on levels of rejection for be-ing different, how easy it is to ask team members for help, and whether tough issues and problems are welcomed into the discussion. Inclusion is just step one, if there's no psychological safety, there's no inclusion[75].

Human beings want to be included. We also want to learn. Then we want to contribute. And finally, we want to challenge the status quo when we believe things need to change. Not being given the right environment to have a voice and essentially being mistreated has a negative impact on our ability to per-form, create value, and thrive.

Making the decision to speak up against a toxic culture is one of the most difficult decisions employees may face in their careers. The way our model and assessment approaches adaptability as a positive opportunity to evolve one's self and the environment creates an opportunity to gather this valuable data input with reduced fear and confrontation. An environment that facilitates safe ways to learn unlocks confidence, resilience, and independence.

In the book *The 4 Stages of Psychological Safety* by Dr Timothy R. Clark, the author expresses a view I agree with in that if you were to conduct a postmortem analysis for almost any commercial organisation, you can trace the cause of death to a lack of challenger safety. And therefore: an environment that stifles adaptability. He further writes where there is no tolerance for candour, there is no constructive dissent. Where there is no constructive dissent, there is no innovation. We must have accurate data as to the levels of team support as the basis to support leaders to foster an environment in which people are given respect and permission to feel included, learn, contribute, and innovate.

Whilst many might desire a culture where there is no stigma, no blame, and no embarrassment associated with failure, it is difficult to know if this exists in the far corners of your company, out of sight. An important signal which might indicate low levels of team support is the leader's response to dissent or bad news. Leaders must model a level of humility and curiosity when new ideas are voiced, for it is a powerful way to foster acceptance. Dr Clark shares a great reality check: "fear-stricken teams give you their hands, some of their heads, and none of their heart." When we can build effective team support we can give rise to a wave of deeper connection and unrivalled performance. He further adds speaking first when you hold positional power softly censors your team.

It is my belief that the demand for leaders and organisations to provide, nurture, and grow high levels of team support is a prerequisite to survive in our exponential environment that rewards constant innovation and adaption. One of the top five reasons for individuals who chose to stay at a job is working with people who trust and care for one another (48 %)[76]. The level of trust in and care for teammates contributes to the perception of team support which reinforces or weakens organisational adaptability. The greater the team support, the more quickly belonging, engagement, and ability to deal with stress can improve.

IN FACT, WE HAVE FOUND THAT AN INCREASE IN TEAM SUPPORT DECREASES WORK STRESS BY 28%. IT WAS THE SECOND MOST EFFECTIVE BUFFER AGAINST STRESS, AFTER RESILIENCE ABILITY.

LOW TEAM SUPPORT

"BEST KEEP YOUR HEAD DOWN AROUND HERE"

→ Feel team is competitive with one way of doing things

→ See sharing new ideas as risky

→ Be less likely to ask peers for help

→ Believe past mistakes are held against you

→ Avoid raising up problems and challenges

→ Feel individual ideas are rejected

MEDIUM TEAM SUPPORT

"I ENJOY SHARING WITH A FEW CLOSE-KNIT COLLEAGUES"

→ Share challenges with close colleagues

→ Avoid showing/expressing true self

→ Be open, but with some caution

→ Promote lower risk options

→ At times, feel safe to experiment

→ Be okay with asking for help

HIGH TEAM SUPPORT

"I CAN BE MY WHOLE -SELF WITHOUT FEAR"

→ Highly experimental, mistakes are not held against you

→ Very comfortable in asking for help

→ Take greater risks

→ Share openly different views and ideas

→ Bring up tough issues without judgement

→ Experience radical team transparency

14. WORK ENVIRONMENT

In the context of our AQ model and assessment, Work Environment does not represent the "physical" workspace, but the systems, processes, and methodologies in place around you which relate to when people adapt. Does your organisation facilitate and encourage self-disruption, rapid experimentation, and regular adaption, or does it hamper them? Is experimentation and alternative thinking formally **rewarded and encouraged,** with clear processes for this to take place? Whilst some employees might report an open and honest, "psychologically safe" space within their teams, this sub-dimension expands to encompass aspects of the organisational system as a whole, considering data inputs around the following five areas:

→ 1. REWARDS: THE LEVEL IN WHICH MY COMPANY/ ORGANISATION REWARDS SOMEONE FOR SHARING NEW IDEAS OR SOLUTIONS.

→ 2. OBSERVABLE ACTS: THE DEGREE TO WHICH SOMEONE OBSERVES OTHER PEOPLE SHARING NEW IDEAS OR SOLUTIONS EVEN IF THEY CONTRAST WITH ESTABLISHED KNOWLEDGE OR WAYS OF DOING.

→ 3. PUNISHMENT: THE OFTEN SUBTLE AND SYSTEMIC CULTURAL IMPACTS, WHERE SOMEONE FEELS THEIR COMPANY WILL HOLD IDEAS OR SOLUTIONS THAT "FAIL" AGAINST THOSE WHO CREATED OR CHAMPIONED THEM.

→ 4. SPACE, PROCESS AND FORUMS: THE LEVEL OF AN ORGANISATIONAL PROCESS WHERE OPEN DISCUSSIONS CAN TAKE PLACE WHEN VIEWS ARE AT ODDS WITH THE ONES OF OTHER COLLEAGUES, WITH A SPECIFIC PROCESS FOR THE COMPANY TO ENCOURAGE COUNTERINTUITIVE AND DIVERGENT THINKING.

→ 5. PUBLIC CELEBRATION: WHEN MISTAKES HAPPEN, ARE THEY ROUTINELY HIDDEN OR OPENLY DISCUSSED? WITH A COMPANY-WIDE ARENA FOR PAST FAILURES TO BE OPENLY SHARED, ENCOURAGED, AND ADDRESSED IN PUBLIC AS A CELEBRATION.

We see a beneficial work environment for adaptability when any failures are truly seen and shared as opportunities to learn beyond a "closed loop" of one given team and are openly given a place and space across an entire organisation. Consider the power and open source learning from a project created by Code Ogden, "Killed By Google": ***https://killedbygoogle.com/*** It is known as the Google graveyard, a free and open source list of discontinued Google services, products, devices, and apps, with the aim to be a source of factual information about the history surrounding Google's dead projects. Contributors from around the world help compile, research, and maintain information about dying and dead Google products.

Let's look at the different types of work environments on this sub-dimension scale. First, let's understand how a **"Closed & Pragmatic"** environment affects adaptability.

People working in this environment are likely to feel afraid and do not regularly share new ideas or knowledge across the organisation, especially if it challenges established viewpoints. Employees believe it is risky to engage in counterintuitive thinking or experimentation as mistakes are held against them, punished, or perceive that they would be negatively affected. What we see here is people believing it is better to keep past failures or mistakes quiet rather than dissecting and discussing them, missing out on the opportunity to learn from them. As a result, adaptability is in silos, and often small, incremental, and very slow—if it takes place at all. Breakthroughs are rare and innovation is hampered. Closed and pragmatic environments foster a protective mindset, with an increase in anxiety and an uplift in workplace stress as a result.

People who score in the mid-range of this scale are not comfortable sharing new or radical ideas or ways of working in public. However, there may be an avenue to do so within their team. People experiencing this are often frustrated as it can feel like their suggestions are stifled by bureaucracy and not able to benefit everyone.

An optimal work environment for accelerated adaptability is an **"Open & Experimental"** one.

People feel they can openly share new ideas or knowledge across their whole company, as they are welcome to give input even if it is challenging established ways of working. There are systems in place to reward new ideas, and share "failures". They strongly believe counterintuitive thinking and experimentation are encouraged. Mistakes are not held against them or their colleagues. As a result, they know it is safe to share past failures in public and are willing to discuss solutions openly.

LOW WORK ENVIRONMENT - CLOSED AND PRAGMATIC

"THE WAY WE DO THINGS TEND TO STAY THE SAME AROUND HERE"

→ **Believe colleagues regularly hide mistakes**

→ **Feel afraid, and avoid company-wide sharing of new ideas**

→ **See counterintuitive thinking as too risky**

→ **Fear negative outcomes**

→ **Keep failures quiet, breakthroughs are rare**

→ **Experience slow adaption, often in silos**

MEDIUM WORK ENVIRONMENT

"WE COULD DO SO MUCH MORE IF WE SHARED"

→ **Share with team, but not organisation**

→ **Feel frustrated**

→ **Struggle with ineffective processes**

→ **Feel ideas are stifled by bureaucracy**

→ Experience blockages to progress

→ See breakthroughs as happenstance

HIGH WORK ENVIRONMENT - OPEN AND EXPERIMENTAL

"I'M ALWAYS LEARNING FROM OTHERS"

→ Be rewarded for sharing new ideas

→ Feel actively encouraged to pursue out of the box thinking

→ Openly discuss mistakes across the whole organisation

→ Have confidence in your organisations experimentation processes

→ Emboldened to disrupt existing processes

→ Feel empowered and experience more innovation breakthroughs

15. WORK STRESS

We measure work stress as the sense of task overwhelm within your organisation. A feeling of too much work and expectation at the extreme can limit employees' adaptability as they will not have the adequate cognitive or time resources to effectively deal with change. This dimension, like many in our model, is based upon existing research. Drawn in part from the Occupational Stress Inducers(OSI) (Which in full has some 46 questions in itself), we focussed on OSI Category I Intrinsic to job / Contextual factors[77], workload, and work pressure[78].

It is important to note that the absence of work stress can also have a negative effect on adaption. With an overt feeling of comfort, the imperative to adapt is diminished. With very high levels one can often feel paralyzed, numb, and at risk of burnout. Therefore a balance of **"healthy stress", called "EUSTRESS" is good.** Eustress was coined by endocrinologist Hans Selye, consisting of the Greek prefix *eu-* meaning "good", and stress, literally meaning "good stress".

The Stress Curve:

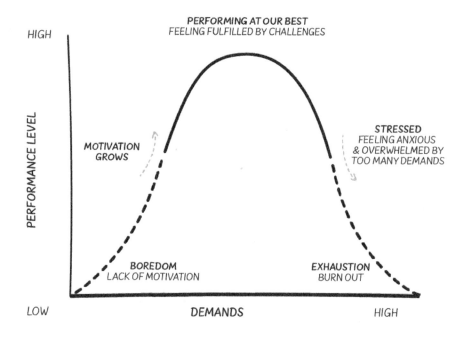

SOURCE: MINDWELL-LEEDS.ORG[79]

Work stress is a critically important indicator to understand, track, and optimally harness. Navigating and dealing with uncertainty for many increases anxiety, and can have significant negative physical, social, and even financial impacts. What are the insights for people who report high levels of work stress? In the simplest terms, they believe the level of work expected of them is overwhelming, regularly experiencing high stress when continually feeling unable to finish their daily tasks. They might describe a sinking feeling as new tasks keep piling up and believe it is too much work for one person.

High work stress over the long term can lead to higher employee turnover[80], poor sleep[81], sickness, and burnout.

People with a midpoint and balanced level of work stress are generally in what we describe as a healthy zone, as we need an element of stress to grow, adapt, and change. This level of healthy stress ensures that deadlines are hit, together with growth and innovation continuing at a good pace. Work stress can change very quickly, so be careful that overwhelm has and might again creep in during busy times.

People with low levels of reported work stress are confident that they can handle their work demands. Sure they can finish all required tasks while adequately addressing new tasks that come in. Expected work is in line with their time and capabilities to achieve. Long-term, low-stress levels mean a greater likelihood they will experiment, try new things, and are less likely to be absent due to stress.

However, remember very low or complete absence of any work stress can have a negative effect on adaption. The more comfortable we are, the less we feel the need to change.

LOW WORK STRESS

"I HAVE SPACE FOR NEW THINGS"

→ Can handle your daily workload

→ Experience low levels of work stress

→ Have the capacity for new work and tasks

→ Feel workload expectations is manageable

→ Be able to finish tasks you start

→ Have less risk of stress-related absenteeism

MEDIUM WORK STRESS

"I'M OKAY, AT THE MOMENT"

→ Drive change and innovation

→ Hit deadlines, most of the time

→ Have a healthy level of workplace stress

→ Moments of overload, but soon passes

→ Have time to experiment with new tasks

→ Feel you have space to think

HIGH WORK STRESS

"I SIMPLY HAVE TOO MUCH FOR ONE PERSON TO DO"

→ Feel there are too many tasks to do

→ Unable to finish your daily tasks

→ 'Sinking' feeling, and missed deadlines

→ Feel expectations are too high

→ Feel stressed and lack time for new things ·
Be at risk of burnout

EXERCISE 6:

Phew! That was a lot of information to absorb! Let's bring it back to basics.

FROM THE LIST OF THE FIFTEEN SUB-DIMENSIONS OF AQ CIRCLE THREE YOU THINK YOU ARE STRONG IN AND STAR ONE THAT YOU THINK MIGHT BE AN OPPORTUNITY TO DEVELOP FOR YOU.

1. GRIT

2. MENTAL FLEXIBILITY

3. MINDSET

4. RESILIENCE

5. UNLEARNING

6. EMOTIONAL RANGE

7. EXTRAVERSION PREFERENCE

8. HOPE

9. MOTIVATION STYLE

10. THINKING STYLE

11. COMPANY SUPPORT

12. EMOTIONAL HEALTH

13. TEAM SUPPORT

14. WORK ENVIRONMENT

15. WORK STRESS

Do you notice a concentration in a particular dimension (such as AQ-Ability, AQ-Character, or AQ-Environment).

KNOW THYSELF

An old Latin maxim advised temet nosce or "know thyself". Without awareness, without self-insight, we cannot change.

But it's worth bearing in mind we may not need to change as much as we think. At AQai, we prefer to view adaptability or AQ as a continuum, not a black-or-white ultimatum. When we say that "the future belongs to those who train their adaptability muscle" we don't mean that those who score low on "resilience" on our AQme diagnostic will be cast into the fire! We all have different abilities, different strengths and weaknesses, and indeed studies have shown that diverse teams (including not just ethnic, racial, or gender diversity but also cognitive diversity) perform better than homogenous ones[82]. An AQme profile should always be viewed within the context of both the individual's and organisation's goals and objectives. A profile that, for example, is more change-averse might be very useful in a situation where very precise, error-free labour is required (for example, one would be reassured if a surgeon did not take unnecessary risks!).

In creating our AQ assessment, we engaged in extensive research, validation, and balancing innovation and new ideas about AQ with studies and evidence. We spent 2 years researching **hundreds of studies, collaborating with universities**, professors, and leaders in psychology, people analytics, and human behaviour **to build a robust and accurate measure of human adaptability** in the workplace. We are continually conducting deeper research, and have multiple partnerships, including one with IE Business School and IE University in Spain.

Though our tool is based on extensive research, we also recognise there is a balance to be struck between the academic world of research and the practical world of lived experience. Author M. J. Ryan draws on the experience of Aikido to outline three requisites of success: "mastery with self", "mastery with others," and "mastery with change". You can see how this aligns almost alarmingly neatly with our tripartite model of adaptability! Sometimes, you have to "live it"—to fight in the dojo—in order to truly know.

This is reflected in our AQme diagnostic itself: 30% of its content was constructed in relation to information and research obtained from interviews with contemporary, top-level HR professionals, leading authors, and pioneering thought leaders rather than peer-reviewed academic studies. You might view this as an example of Unlearning in action. The sheer rapidity of new information necessitates a constant awareness and monitoring of whether our current data set or methodology is viable, working, and providing value. Science in its truest sense has no relation to judgement. No expectation or bias. It is a pure hypothesis, equally allowing for disproof as well as proof.

YOU ARE NOT YOUR JOB

Now that you have a much deeper understanding of the fundamentals of AQ, you can truly begin your adaptability journey. It's worth reminding one here that our ability to navigate change is released by letting go of our role as identity.

Earlier we discussed not self-identifying with our emotions. This also applies to the idea of having a single "role" in society, or at any given time. The issue of flexibility in regard to the way we work, how we work, where we work, and more, is one that is of growing prevalence. In fact what we define as "work" is evolving and adapting. Covid-19 has thrown to light that the paradigms of working at an office, in a specific locale, are becoming increasingly redundant. Likewise, many people are still in the mindset of singular careers, doing specific activities, for a living, with which they identify. Aka, "I am an accountant." No, you are a human being who is skilled in and chose accountancy work! This correlates with step 1 of unlocking your AQ potential as a leader: decoupling yourself from your "role" or "label". Many people place all their bets on one profession, one skill, or one expertise. Their education is about focus - a major - and it prepares them for application in a defined field. They continue to upskill, to drive greater and greater experience, responsibility, and reward. Often driving to the same office, they do the same routine tasks, and after a set or allotted amount of time, they expect to earn a promotion. This is the world they knew, a world that existed for millennia, but that has changed.

When technology disrupts a profession, making a given skill redundant, or democratises expertise online, we are back to square one, and it can feel for some people like their whole life has collapsed. We're no longer in that linear world of doing "one thing". The world is moving too fast for that.

Increasingly, we're moving to portfolio careers, where we embrace multiple professional paths simultaneously. Once frowned on as "moon-lighting", now it has been reframed as "side hustles". But I believe this can go way beyond "character-building" and is an opportunity for a true explosion of fulfilment when it is a case of someone pursuing multiple interests in a balanced fashion. Of course, this is different to one person having to work three jobs just to pay bills. In that instance, something needs to change.

We cannot adapt if we don't change. To change, we must be flexible. And in today's exponential world, we have to be flexible in just about every walk of life.

The modern world places increasing demands on our time, so we need to be able to evaluate and make decisions in a hyper-contextual way. For example, we might need to be able to run a current business process whilst also searching for ways the model can be improved, transformed, and perhaps completely disrupted, a duality made possible through understanding the need for contextualisation and the mental flexibility to support seemingly opposing demands.

So, we must be prepared to be flexible in how we work, rather than rigid. In the words of Maria Matarelli: "What I've found is that those who approach their projects with a rigid system often buckle under the shifting currents of the market."

Ken Wilber described this as "the Ego Level" of consciousness in his book *The Spectrum of Consciousness:* "the Ego Level is what you feel when you feel yourself to be a father, a mother, a lawyer, a businessman, an American, or any other particular role of image." However, by limiting ourselves to these self-and-societally created roles, we can sometimes do more harm than good: "on the Ego Level... dualism-repression-projection severs the psyche, represses its essential unity, and thus creates the unconscious Shadow—all of the re-pressed traits and wishes that the ego has attempted to vanquish by pushing them out of consciousness."

The time has come to take the leap and decouple your sense of Self from your "job" or what you perceive to be your role in life. Our research into AQ-Ability, AQ-Character, and AQ-Environment reveals that we are far more pliable than we think. Even our personalities, perhaps perceived by many to be set in stone—or at least written in pen and not pencil—are in fact changeable, and deeper research into neuroplasticity is revealing the countless ways we can rewire our brains.

No one embodies this philosophy more than Mary Lou Jepson. She is an inventor, technologist, and expert in the field of VR, holograms, imaging, and the fields of display. She has worked for many organisations over her career, including Google X and Facebook / Oculus. Her current project is called OpenWater. Founded in 2016, OpenWater is creating fMRI-type imaging of the body using infrared. It will essentially revolutionise the medical world and MRI scans by converting a machine the size of a small room into something held in the palm of the hand. Long term, her aims are to use it for surgery without an incision and brain-to-computer communication.

In 1995, Jepson suffered from a pituitary gland tumour. Aged twenty-nine, she was confined to a wheelchair and suffered headaches that would block out all else. After an MRI, the tumour was removed, but as a result of the gland being taken out, she now suffers from panhypopituitarism (her body produces no hormones), requiring a strict regimen of hormone replacement. She has had to adapt her whole way of life to accommodate this condition.

Of special relevance to our point about identity, Jepson's tumour occurred midway through her PhD. She says: "There's a stigma when you undergo brain surgery. Are you still smart or not? So afterwards I tried to challenge myself to find out." Rather than allowing herself to be defined by her condition, she finished her course in the next six months and then co-founded MicroDisplay, a company that manufactures liquid-crystal-on-silicon chips for high-definition TV displays.

In 2003 Jepson left MicroDisplay and in 2005 joined MIT Media Lab as a tenure-track professor. She started the Nomadic Displays Group. Now we see a radical shift, again demonstrating an openness to new learning, new experiences, new altruism and new opportunities unbounded by the idea of a "niche role". Jepson co-founded One Laptop Per Child with Nicholas Negroponte. The aim of One Laptop Per Child (OLPC), was to create a $100 computer, with the lowest-power laptop ever made, and distribute them to children in the developing world. Via OLPC, millions of units have shipped to children in over fifty countries and in more than twenty-five different languages. Jepsen invented the laptop's sunlight-readable display technology and had a hand in its ultra-low power management system.

It's worth pointing out here that in the West we have a very limited view of learning. If you want to find out something or deepen your understanding, you go to an academic institution. The institution uses researchers and studies in order to validate what they teach: over many decades, sometimes even centuries. When you study at a university or academic institution, you are taught how things "have previously been done", because these "tried and trusted" methods are the ones that are validated.

I'm not disparaging the value of academic research or researchers. In fact, we ourselves are working closely with researchers to continually improve and validate our findings. Learning the historical contexts for what you're trying to achieve is also key. It allows us to avoid the mistakes of the past and to better understand our present. However, it is limiting to think that the only way we can learn, and the only place we can learn, is through an academic institution. Mary Lou Jepson has gone beyond academia, learning through *doing, collaborations*, and through real-world *experimentation*. The power of leveraging situational context, shifting from lab to life.

As Singularity University alumni, there was an interesting conversation about how the university's learning modules and curriculums were set up in the early days. At first, they had great difficulty in gaining validation from academic bodies, because traditionally, academic institutions needed to teach subjects and concepts that have a clear curriculum with solid structures sustained over a number of years. Singularity University, of course, specialises in scientific progress and exponential technology. It sits at the cutting edge. What may have been part of a curriculum a year ago is almost certainly not true now, because some wild innovation or invention has disrupted it. So, how to achieve a reputable academic or university status when, in an ideal world, Singularity University would change its course content every year, perhaps even more frequently! We are going to soon have to adapt our thinking about what constitutes robust and valuable education in the realm of scientific endeavour, research, and more.

When we consider learning in the workplace, historically we tended to ask questions like:

DOES SOMEONE HAVE A DRIVE TO CONTINUALLY LEARN? AND, HOW CAN WE IMPROVE AND BOLSTER THAT DRIVE?

However, it's worth pointing out that there is a deeper question:

WHY ARE WE DRIVEN TO LEARN?

I think each of us might have a unique answer to that question.

A tumour changed Mary Lou Jepson's life, and now she is creating something with OpenWater that can detect tumours with pinpoint accuracy, and what's more, that is completely non-invasive. She is rethinking the existing models, using something as simple as light to map the human body and brain. In her April 2018 TEDTalk, you can see her unpacking the creative process of arriving at infrared as a way of creating fMRIs. It is playful, and at times, even bizarre. She holds up a piece of raw chicken meat with a tumour implanted in it and shines an infrared light on the other side. We can see the tumour. Then she shows us that light can even travel through bone, by using a shard of a real human skull that she "ordered from SkullsUnlimited.com".

Each experiment gets us further to understand how this might actually work. Every experiment teaches us something new. There is an effervescent joy to the process of discovery. We're told that traditional MRI scanners can only image to one-millimetre thickness. Jepson's light system can image to two-thousandths of a millimetre (two microns). The smallest neuron in the human brain has a diameter of two microns, as it happens, making her system orders of magnitude more precise and useful.

Undoubtedly hard work creates breakthroughs. But I wonder whether the most significant breakthroughs are created by this playful, joyous experimentation. That's another way we might have to adapt our thinking. The stiff, stuffy, deadly-serious corporate environments are becoming a thing of the past because they are not conducive to creativity, which is what every organisation is going to need, not in ten years' time, but *now*. The old belief that work was "drudgery" could not be further from the future I am envisioning, and indeed at times living.

Jepson's Unlearning-ability, constant experimentation, and pushing of her own boundaries both physical and mental seems characterised by a child-like wonder, an openness to new possibilities supported and driven by a steadfast commitment to purpose.

Letting go of our "ego", and leaning into this liberating release of self-imposed identity, can lead us to a bigger, bolder future than we could ever imagine.

EXERCISE 8:

WRITE DOWN WHAT YOUR "JOB" OR ROLE IS.

....

....

....

....

....

....

....

NOW WRITE DOWN FIVE TO SEVEN OTHER JOBS OR ROLES THAT YOU FEEL EXCITED BY.

....

....

....

....

....

....

....

For example, if you are a CEO, you might write down: leader, speaker, mentor, innovator, and technologist. Now imagine what it would be like to add five or six more!

WOULD YOU NEED TO LET GO OF ONE OF THE OLD ROLES TO MAKE ROOM FOR A NEW ONE OR COULD YOU EXPAND TO INCLUDE ALL OF THEM?

....

....

....

....

....

HOW MIGHT MULTIPLICATION HAPPEN BY SUBTRACTION, THE SUBTRACTION FROM WHAT WAS, TO THE PATH OF WHAT COULD BE?

....

....

....

....

....

....

SUMMARY FOR PART 2

→ LEADERS MUST NOW STEER THEIR ORGANISATIONS THROUGH A VUCA (VOLATILE, UNCERTAIN, COMPLEX, AMBIGUOUS) WORLD

→ ADAPTABILITY IS ALWAYS CONTEXTUAL; THERE IS NO ABSOLUTE "RIGHT" OR "WRONG"

→ WE MEASURE AQ ACROSS THREE CORE DIMENSIONS: AQ-ABILITY, AQ-CHARACTER, AND AQ-ENVIRONMENT

→ THE SHEER RAPIDITY OF NEW INFORMATION NECESSITATES A CONSTANT AWARENESS AND MONITORING OF WHETHER OUR CURRENT DATA-SET OR METHODOLOGY IS VIABLE AND WORKING

→ THE THIRD STAGE IN THE PYRAMID OF ADAPTABILITY IS TO DECOUPLE OUR IDENTITY FROM A SPECIFIC ROLE, PROFESSION, OR "JOB"

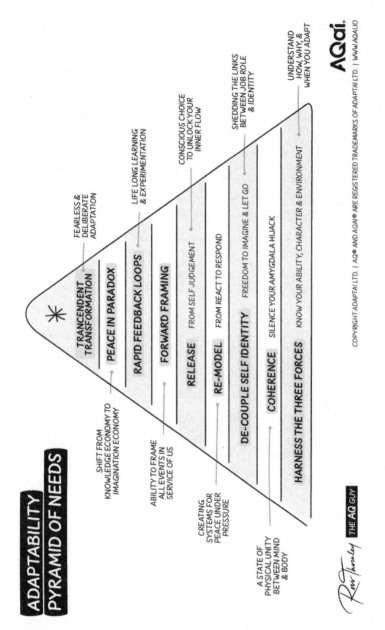

My Adaptability Pyramid of Needs™ shown here again for reference of where we are on the epic adventure of our adaptability intelligence.

1 U.S. Bureau of Labor Statistics; Economic News Release; https://www.bls.gov/news.release/jolts.nr0.htm; July 6, 2022.

2 Spinelli, Steven; CNBC; online: https://www.cnbc.com/2018/02/02/automation-will-kill-1-million-jobs-by-2026-what-we-need-to-do-commentary.html; 2018.

3 Vincent, James; The Verge; online: https://www.theverge.com/2017/11/30/16719092/automation-robots-jobs-global-800-million-forecast; 2017.

4 Bureau of Labor Statistics

5 Defining the skills citizens will need in the future world of work - A survey of 18,000 people in 15 countries - https://www.mckinsey.com/industries/public-and-social-sector/our-insights/defining-the-skills-citizens-will-need-in-the-future-world-of-work

6 https://news.linkedin.com/2019/January/linkedin-releases-2019-global-talent-trends-report

7 Martin, Nejad, Colmar, & Liem, 2013

8 Results of IRT analysis; Source: Conceptual Framework For Meta-Analysis on the Career Construction Model of Adaptation (Savickas, 2005, 2013; Savickas et al., 2009; Savickas & Profeli, 2012)

9 Roberts et al., 2005

10 O'Reilly & Tushman, 2004

11 Junni, Sarala, Taras, & Tarba, 2013

12 O'Reilly III & Tushman, 2008

13 Mind Your Errors : Evidence for a Neural Mechanism Linking Growth Mind-Set to Adaptive Posterror Adjustments; Jason S. Moser, Hans S. Schroder, Carrie Heeter, Tim P. Moran and Yu-Hao Lee; *Psychological Science* 2011 22: 1484 originally published online 31 October 2011 DOI: 10.1177/0956797611419520

14 Tabibnia, G., & Radecki, D. (2018). Resilience training that can change the brain. Consulting Psychology Journal: Practice and Research, 70(1), 59–88

15 Real Strength

16 Description: four influence levers; Source: https://www.mckinsey.com/~/media/mckinsey/business%20functions/organization/our%20insights/leading%20agile%20transformation%20the%20new%20capabilities%20leaders%20need%20to%20build/leading-agile-transformation-the-new-capabilities-leaders-need-to-build-21st-century-organizations.ashx

17 Quoted cited from 1734.

18 (Claridge & Davis, 2001)

19 *Psychologies Magazine; Real Strength;* Capstone; 2017.

20 *The Bright and Dark Sides of Talent At Work*, Oluf Gøtzsche-Astrup, Consulting Psychology Journal, 2018, Vol. 70, No. 2, 167-181.

21 *The New Technologies In Personality Assessment:* A Review, Zohra Ihsan, Adrian Furnham, Consulting Psychology Journal, 2018, Vol. 70, No. 2, 147-166.

22 (Snyder et al. 1991, p. 287)

23 (see Snyder 2000 and Lopez 2013 for comprehensive reviews)

24 Snyder et al., 1991

25 Snyder, 1994a, 1994b

26 Snyder, 2002

27 Bandura, 1977

28 Scheier & Carver, 1985

29 Rand, 2009

30 Snyder et al., 1991

31, 33, 35, 37 Snyder et al., 1996

32 Snyder, Feldman, Shorey, & Rand, 2002

34 Davidson, Feldman, & Margalit, 2012

36 Gustafsson, Hassmén, & Podlog, 2010

38 Peterson, Gerhardt, & Rode, 2006

39 Davidson et al., 2012; Rolo & Gould, 2007

40 Curry, Snyder, Cook, Ruby, & Rehm, 1997

41 Rudolph, C. W., Lavigne, K. N., & Zacher, H. (2017). Career adaptability: A meta-analysis of relationships with measures of adaptivity, adapting responses, and adaptation results. Journal of Vocational Behavior, 98, 17-34.

42 Peterson and Byron 2008
43 Snyder 1999
44 Irving et al. 1998; Luthans et al. 2008; Snyder et al. 2000
45 https://psycnet.apa.org/record/2012-20778-010 "Can hope be changed in 90 minutes? Testing the efficacy of a single-session goal-pursuit intervention for college students."
46 Snyder 2000
47 Pizer and Haertel 2006
48 Higgins, 1997
49 Zhou et al. 2017; Johnson et al., 2015
50 TIll Nicolas Deuschel, Jill Waymire Paine, and Jing Zhou, 2018 : Solving Complexities in Creativity Research: Towards a Holistic Understanding across Levels
51 Lanaj et al. 2012
52 e.g. Crowe & Higgins, 1997
53 Johnson, Chang & Yang, 2010
54 Higgins, 1997
55 Zhou et al. 2017; Kammerlander, Burger, Fust & Fueglistaller, 2015; Baas et al. 2011; Roese, Hur & Pennington 1999
56 Psychologies Magazine; *Real Strength*; Capstone; 2017.
57 Quoted in *The Spectrum of Consciousness;* Wilber, Ken; 1977.
58 Melrona Kirrane, Margaret Lennon, Cliodhna O'Connor & Na Fu; "Linking perceived management support with employees' readiness for change: the mediating role of psychological capital'" 2016.
59 Breevaart et al.,2014; Morgeson & Humphrey, 2006; Nielsen, Randall, Yarker, & Brenner, 2008; Piccolo & Colquitt, 2006; Podsakoff, MacKenzie, & Bommer, 1996; Rhoades & Eisenberger, 2002; Skakon, Nielsen, Borg, & Guzman, 2010; Van Dierendonck & Jacobs, 2012; Whittington, Goodwin, & Murray, 2004
60 Jimmieson, White, & Zajdlewicz, 2009.
61 Bouckenooghe et al., 2009; Dirk & Ferrin, 2002.
62 Gardner, Cogliser, Davis, & Dickens, 2011.
63 Detert & Bruno, in press.
64 Avolio & Gardner, 2005.
65 Luthans & Avolio, 2003: 243.
66 "The impact of the prolonged COVID-19 pandemic on stress resilience and mental health: A critical review across waves"; Mirko Manchia,a,b,c Anouk W. Gathier,d Hale Yapici-Eser,e,f Mathias V. Schmidt,g Dominique de Quervain,hTherese van Amelsvoort,i Jonathan I. Bisson,j John F. Cryan,k Oliver D. Howes,l Luisa Pinto,m,nNic J. van der Wee,o Katharina Domschke,p,q Igor Branchi,r and Christiaan H. Vinkerss,t,*' Eur Neuropsychopharmacol.; PMC PubMed Central; Feb 2022;
67 CAA Airport Data 2021". caa.co.uk. UK Civil Aviation Authority. 15 April 2022.
68 Air Transport Action Group Study 2022
69 https://seamilano.eu/en/financial-information
70 Cirium data and analytics
71 International Airport Review
72 Jobs search engine Adzuna
73 Christine Porath, Gretchen Spreitzer, Cristina Gibson, Flannery G. Garnett (2011) Thriving at work: Toward its measurement, construct validation, and theoretical refinement. Journal of Organisational Behaviour. Pages 250-275
74 Spreitzer, G. & Porath, C. (2012) Creating sustainable Performance. Harvard Business Review
75 The 4 Stages of Psychological Safety" by Dr Timothy R. Clark
76 McKinsey The Great Attrition: The power of adaptability
77 Card, H.L.(2002): Evers, Frese, and Cooper (2000); Morimoto(2006) ; Imrab et al(2013)
78 Card, H.L.(2002); Islam and Munir (2011): Usman Ali et al (2014);Manzoor, Awan&Mariam(2011)
79 Dodson, J. D. (1915). The relation of strength of stimulus to rapidity of habit-formation in the kitten. Journal of Animal Behavior, 5(4), 330
80 Nina Gupta, Terry A. Beehr, Job stress and employee behaviors, Organizational Behavior and Human Performance,
Volume 23, Issue 3, 1979, Pages 373-387,

81 Eui-Joong Kim & Joel E. Dimsdale (2007) The Effect of Psychosocial Stress on Sleep: A Review of Polysomnographic Evidence, Behavioral Sleep Medicine, 5:4, 256-278, DOI: 10.1080/15402000701557383

82 McKinsey & Company 2015 report "Diversity Matters"

PART 3: HARNESS THE THREE FORCES

THE POWER OF STORYTELLING

Parts 1 and 2 of this book introduced the importance of adaptability and the theory behind AQ. Now, we move to the **how** of not just becoming more adaptable as individuals but improving the adaptability of our teams, organisations, and—let's shoot for the moon—even our societies!

Each sub-dimension of AQ is a life's work to understand and improve. Angela Duckworth's recent book entitled *Grit* is a testament to that fact! This means it can be daunting to know where to start. The temptation is to dive immediately into our weakest sub-dimension (for example, perhaps we have low Resilience), and then frantically begin trying to improve it.

However, this is a *reaction*, not a response!

The first thing we need to do is start with the three main dimensions: AQ-Ability, AQ-Character, and AQ-Environment. If we understand how these "three forces" interrelate, then we can leverage the best results for ourselves and for our teams.

To start with, we have to recognise that we can leverage each of these three forces, not just AQ-Ability. Our society is built around the concept that our character is fixed, but as Dr Benjamin Hardy observed, "Personality is a skill." The notion that our personality is fixed is extremely limiting, it puts us on railroad tracks so we can't deviate from our course, even if the railroad runs out or if there's a huge obstacle in the way!

Likewise, many have a notion that our environments are fixed and we have to move out of challenging environments–aka, leave a stressful job, or change the industry our business operates in–when things go wrong or get uncomfortable. The reality, however, is that our environments are ever-shifting. Not only this, but we are the curators of our environment. We create an environment in which we then invite other people to cohabitate. Not just as business leaders, but in our day-to-day lives. And yes, to a degree, our choice of an environment may be limited by—for example—financial resources. But even if we cannot afford a mansion or a humongous office space, we can make the most of the space we have; this is saying nothing of the psychological environment we create: is it one of trust, mutual respect, and openness to all views and ideas? In my view, our environment can be either the "magical multiplier" of success or its great subtractor.

So, it's only by utilising all three of these dimensions that we can achieve a breakthrough and unlock our adaptability potential. We must:

→ **HARNESS OUR ABILITIES**

→ **KNOW OUR CHARACTER**

→ **CURATE OUR ENVIRONMENT**

HARNESS OUR ABILITIES

Every day of our lives, we tell ourselves stories. Unfortunately, due to our cognitive bias, most of these stories tend to be negative. On a day-to-day basis, we tell ourselves: "I'm not very organised", or, "I never win.", or "I'm not very good with technology." These narratives, repeated over long periods, begin to develop power over us, and we hypnotise ourselves into believing them to be true when in fact they more often than not have very little basis in reality. Psychologists refer to these narratives as "self-limiting beliefs", and we all have them to a degree. The key is not to let them control us, to constantly challenge these beliefs.

THIS IS THE ONLY WAY WE CAN BREAK THROUGH THE ILLUSIONARY CAGE WE HAVE CREATED FOR OURSELVES.

We don't necessarily have to jump in at the deep-end. If your narrative is that you're terrified of heights, and this fear/belief is limiting your way of life (because, for example, it's preventing you from going on holiday to the places you want to), I am not suggesting you jump out of an aeroplane and skydive! There are lots of smaller steps one can take on a more regular, day-to-day basis which will have the effect of gradually chipping away at the belief, to begin the journey of unlearning and rewiring your thoughts. Rather than trying to smash it down in one go. These beliefs have been built up over a long time, remember, so it is unlikely any experience, no matter how awesome or awe-inspiring, will rewrite them wholesale. The process of steadily challenging them every day, however, could just chip away at the stonework and allow you out of the prison cell, much like Andy Dufresne in *Shawshank Redemption*.

In the book *Real Strength*, published by Psychologies Magazine, the authors describe a study conducted in the late 1980s by James Pennebaker, a psychological researcher at the University of Texas in Austin. The experiment was conducted on 50 healthy undergraduates. The group was split into two, with one group asked to write each week for 15 minutes per day, for four days in a row, about "the darkest, most traumatic experience of their lives" whereas the other group was asked to write about "superficial topics" for the same duration. "Six weeks after the writing sessions, students in the trauma group reported more positive moods and fewer illnesses than those writing about everyday experiences. They also reported improved immunity and fewer visits to the health centre. Pennebaker concluded from this experiment that confronting traumatic experiences was physically beneficial."[1] Fifteen minutes a day is all it requires to shift paradigms. As Psychologies Magazine writes, "Analysing their writing, Pennebaker noticed that they were trying to derive meaning from the trauma. They probed into the causes and consequences of the adversity and, as a result, eventually grew wiser about it. Interestingly, people who used the exercise to vent received no health benefits. There was something unique about the exercise of actual storytelling that helped people to find meaning and a silver lining."

EXERCISE 9:

WRITE DOWN THREE THINGS YOU BELIEVE TO BE TRUE ABOUT YOURSELF.

1. ....

....

2. ....

....

3. ....

....

Try to do this unconsciously and quickly without allowing your rational brain to interfere or "correct" your responses.

In Part 5 we'll cover another exercise that can help us build our adaptability muscles even further.

MASS POSITIVE HYSTERIA

Know Our Character

Another important aspect of storytelling is linked to the interconnectedness and virality of modern culture. By this, I mean we are now so aware of what is going on all over the world. This means we see success stories every time we turn on our phones, inspiring if you have the right mindset. However, for many people, this is very depressing. We see people (usually far younger than us!) achieving worldwide fame, huge success, making astronomical sums of money—or alternatively, we see someone making a significant contribution to a cause we care deeply about and we think we've "missed our chance"—and we can feel bitter and resentful of our own lives. This is because the dominant form of progress measurement—in schools, in businesses, in academic institutions, even in our family homes—is "comparative assessment".

SIMPLY PUT, WE'RE CONSTANTLY COMPARING OUR PROGRESS TO THAT OF OTHERS.

It's an old adage that we should not compare ourselves with others, yet our whole society is built around the idea and actively reinforces it at virtually every juncture of our growth and development until it is very deeply ingrained. Students are encouraged to compare test results with their peers. Then there is the matter of how businesses compete with each other. Often sacrificing their focus on their customers and their products, by focusing on each other.

Our initial *reaction* to being overwhelmed by all these success stories pouring into our newsfeed 24/7 might well be to detach and ignore it. However, other than completely removing oneself from the online world, I think it is probably almost impossible. Instead, I believe we need to *respond* by shifting from comparison to *inspiration*.

One of the greatest examples of shifting from comparison to inspiration is that of Anousheh Ansari.

When Anousheh Ansari first arrived on American soil at the age of 16, she could only speak Farsi and a little French. She had emigrated from Iran to escape the destructive military conflict there. She describes how war changed her: "It was an experience I believe shaped my life, in that I have always wanted to make sure I can do anything to help people find solutions, that don't involve war and military action, to their problems. Nobody wins at wars; the losers are mostly women and children."

It would have been easy, at this stage, to have compared herself to others and those more fortunate. But instead, she found her passion. The constant in her life was science: "I became enamoured with space when I was 6 or 7. Perhaps it gave me an escape from the reality around me. I also loved science. Everything else around me kept changing: War destroyed everything, people lied and no one could be trusted, but I could trust physics and maths and the scientific process."

This fascination would transform into a determination to reach space. On one level, this is an example of exemplary Grit: Anousheh has maintained a disciplined, rational focus on her goals despite terrifying environmental circumstances as a child and young woman. Then subsequently had to adapt to a whole new world when she moved to America (she describes feeling like "an alien on another planet" during her early time in America).

On the other hand, Anousheh describes her interest in space and the determination to get there as being born out of *escapism*. It shows that our environment catalysts our adaptation in several ways. Anousheh perceived the unreliability of the world around her, a world shifting with conflict and betrayal, and latched on to the rigour of the scientific process. Again, rather than focusing on what other people were doing, she chose to direct her focus toward the empirical and the things within her control.

She graduated from George Washington University with a Master of Science in electrical engineering a few years later, having learned English and a range of other skills from teachers she "will always be grateful for".

In 2006, she founded Prodea Systems, an IoT company. This was not her first company, but perhaps her most successful. However, she would achieve the thing she would become best known for later that year.

Anousheh received an offer to train as a backup crew member at the Russian Space Agency for the Soyuz TMA-9 mission. During her training, crew member Daisuke Enomoto developed a medical condition and was disqualified from the flight. Anousheh was able to join the team and fly to the International Space Station, commencing an eleven-day space expedition. She is the world's first female private space explorer and the first Muslim in space. She achieved her ambition, having dreamed of this moment from six years old.

Did space live up to her expectations?

She describes the moment, shared by many world-famous astronauts, of looking down at Earth from over one million feet: "Seeing the Earth from above was an incredibly life-changing experience. From space, Earth has no countries or borders. You truly see the planet as one home we all share together, and you see its fragility. That profoundly changes the way you see the world. You become one with the entire human race at that moment."

It's interesting that her journey has been from an environment of division, barriers, conflict, and territorial boundaries, to one of enlightenment and perspective: despite being surrounded by conflict, she has shown perseverance and Grit, pursuing a journey toward transcendence. She has climbed the mountain, quite literally, and now can look down over the harmony of the valley with new eyes.

Anousheh has founded five businesses and earned multiple international distinctions. Now, she wants to mobilize $1 billion to support female-founded companies. The data shows that "women CEOs actually perform better in terms of outcomes and success and profitability of the companies they found." Studies have shown that businesses founded by women yield double the revenue of those founded by men and then some, yet they receive less than 2% of venture capital investments. And it's not just financial performance. "In designing technologies, when women get involved, the designs are suitable for the entire population, and not only for people who fit the mould of the white man. Perhaps most importantly, women founders focus on services and technology that go beyond profit. They also look at the impact of a product on society, its meaningfulness for humanity..." Anousheh says. This also shows generosity and inspiration. Rather than trying to "hoard" success, she shares it with others. The mindset is not one of scarcity but abundance and hope.

Anousheh Ansari perceives a great many obstacles to the progress of women, from entrenched societal viewpoints (ironically shared by East and West) to risk-aversion that comes from a focus on perfectionism over progress. However, "The greatest barrier for us women is our mindset."

The world is changing rapidly, and it's my belief that game-changers and inspirational role models like Anousheh will pave the way for a better future for women and humankind.

We must learn to adapt, not just in terms of adopting new technology or business practices. Still, we must adapt to help our fellow human beings, to redress inequalities, and to challenge institutional biases and bigotry. And if that means shaking our society's foundations to its core, then we may just have to do it. It will require grit and determination to do it.

But then, doesn't everything worth achieving?

The stories of people like Anousheh Ansari, Mary Lou Jepson, and others do not diminish our own achievements, they only add to them. This is because we are humankind, a collective, a sum of many parts—and at our best, we are one. Our achievements are collective, and we see this in the process of great inventors, composers, creators, and game-changers who build on the achievements of those who went before them.

THEREFORE, ALL SUCCESSES BELONG TO ALL OF US. WE ARE A SPECIES AND THUS ONE PERSON'S INNOVATION IS ALL OF OUR GAINS, especially in our exponential age where knowledge can be so rapidly shared. To take this to an almost non-dualistic and esoteric level: think of that person as you. We were all one in the first atom. Yes, we now inhabit many bodies, but in the beginning, we were all part of one microscopic reality containing no divisions, separations, or "dualities". So, if someone you admire has climbed a mountain, you have also climbed it; there's no need for you to compete with them, simply be inspired and if you so choose, climb one too. The achievement belongs to all. Likewise, if you can play the piano beautifully, so can they. Our relationship with our fellow human beings is a two-way reciprocity of shared success.

Embracing this all-encompassing perspective is, of course, not easy. At times the illusory separateness we feel can be reinforced by those who are less willing to adopt a universal perspective. However, by beginning to see the achievements of others as not cause for begrudgement and competition, but as cause for celebration, **WE CAN SHIFT OUR MINDSET FROM COMPETITION TO COLLABORATION.**

To drive my point home, the collaborative, or perhaps a better phrase would be "co-elevating", mindset I have just described is underpinned by AQ-character. What motivates us, the way we think, our propensity for optimism and hope, all of these influence our ability to access this essentially transcendental mindset. And not only that, but our AQ-Character influences the route towards this goal. We have to know and understand who we are before we can reach this place of peace, where we no longer feel competitive. For example, those with a "play to win" Motivational style may find it difficult not to be competitive, because they feel that burning ambition to achieve their goals. Someone with a "play to protect" Motivational style, on the other hand, might find it easier. There is no one way, or one road, but knowing our character gives us the best possible chance of discovering the path that works for us.

As I mentioned before, our society is built on the notion of competition. This derives from the earliest epochs of humankind in which resources were seen as scarce and therefore had to be hoarded and protected. Anyone who tried to come and take our resources had to be, well, jabbed with a pointy stick.

Our current world, however, is abundant. There is more than enough to go around. In his book *Abundance: The Future Is Better Than You Think*, Peter Diamandis demonstrates analogously how the myth of scarcity is reinforced, "History's littered with tales of once-rare resources made plentiful by innovation. The reason is pretty straightforward: scarcity is often contextual. Imagine a giant orange tree packed with fruit. If I pluck all the oranges from the lower branches, I am effectively out of accessible fruit. From my limited perspective, oranges are now scarce. But once someone invents a new piece of technology called a ladder, I've suddenly got new reach."[2]

I would add to this, not only do we falsely perceive oranges as scarce, but we then erect a picket fence around the tree to stop other people from coming back next winter when the tree bears fruit! We still cling to this old worldview—that resources are scarce and we must protect them—because it's how we've survived. But in our current era, this notion of "scarcity" is often redundant and sometimes actively limiting, as it cuts us off from massive opportunities. I have experienced firsthand the power of collaboration: pooling resources, knowledge, time, ideas, and energy can lead to extraordinary breakthroughs. We build the ladder by working together.

When we collaborate, when we turn away from the rat-race and the primitive notion of competing with everyone and everything, we can unlock our higher purpose: to serve. This also means that we can manifest the best version of ourselves—our true character.

EXERCISE 10:

NAME ONE RESOURCE THAT YOU PREVIOUSLY CONSIDERED TO BE SCARCE BUT WHICH HAS NOW BECOME ABUNDANT.

....

....

....

....

HOW MIGHT THIS NEWFOUND ABUNDANCE CHANGE YOUR FUTURE?

....

....

....

....

....

....

....

....

....

....

Curate Our Environment

Consciously choosing a different environment can be scary because it activates our primitive fear response. Phrases such as "Better the Devil you know" inhibit us because they tie us to existing paradigms. We narrate ourselves into delusions of inadequacy. "I can't climb a mountain," we say. But the reality is: that you already have.

Community, which is a key element of our environment, is a multiplier. However, communities are so powerful that they multiply everything, including our "shadow", to use a Jungian term. We see this evidenced in many highly successful businesses that are blighted by reports of misconduct. The teams are high-performing and get results–it can't be denied. But the pressure-cooker high-stress environment, the image-driven lifestyle, and frequently the "boys' club" mentality, meaning that vices are multiplied along with progress. This is why it is essential that we **DO THE INTERNAL WORK FIRST.**

It's a commonly held truism that sometimes success comes "too early" to some people. Whilst there is likely a good deal of old-fashioned jealousy behind such remarks, it can't be denied that fame and success sadly seem to destroy some people. Usually, this is because **they have not done the internal work; they have not attended to Self.** These fortunate-unfortunate individuals are catapulted into a new environment, new communities, and new realities in which all their unconscious mental detritus is amplified along with their talents and reach. Is it any wonder they collapse?

Take a moment, therefore, to consider your community and your environment. What elements of it serve you? What elements of it do not serve you? Do certain groups encourage habits that are not progressive or useful? Consider what you will deliberately let go of from today.

When measuring results, whether at a personal, team, or organisational level, do we measure how far we've come, or the gap between where we are now and the end goal? Most commonly it's the latter.

As much as I have advocated for letting go of the past—within reason!--results measurement is actually an area where the past can truly serve us.

In Dan Sullivan and Dr Benjamin Hardy's *The Gap and The Gain*, they outline the cultural tendency of the West to focus on the distance between what we have and what we want (the gap), rather than on all that we've accomplished (the gain): "The consequences of this framing aren't small. By embracing the pursuit of happiness, we rob ourselves of happiness in the here and now."[3]

How many meetings start with a dreary assessment of "where we are now", which is invariably short of the objective by some margin? Can we shift this paradigm? As I mentioned before, I open all my meetings with a positive gratitude focus. We look back at where we were and how far we have come. This starts us off on a positive note.

In addition, measuring ourselves against the goal implies our goal is a fixed point (some companies refer to these as "North Stars"). But, in our exponential world, a world in which our ambitions are unfettered, our goals should be constantly growing and shifting as we grow and shift. By fixing the "endpoint" we limit ourselves. Perhaps we should see these as the waypoints, the signposts along the route.

Measuring ourselves against the past frees us from the despair of our seeming lack of progress and the necessity of "fixing" our goals when circumstances or personal growth might dictate they change.

EXERCISE 11:

Take some time here to measure your gains! Approach this through three lenses, over the past 90 days: work, relationships, and self.

WHAT WORK GAINS HAVE YOU MADE?

WHERE WERE YOU AND HOW FAR HAVE YOU COME?

Do this for, your relationships (these could be with friends or your partner)and your personal development (this could be a new hobby you've taken up or an aspect of yourself you're working on, such as weight loss, better sleep, or reading more).

Remember not to measure how far you are to your goal—disregard that entirely for the purpose of this exercise.

Work gains:...
....
....
....
....
....
....
....
....

Relationship gains: ....

....

....

....

....

....

....

Self gains: ....

....

....

....

....

....

BY MEASURING WHERE YOU WERE TO HOW FAR YOU HAVE COME - WHAT ARE YOUR STRATEGIC INSIGHTS IN DOING THIS.

....

....

....

....

....

FROM JUDGEMENT TO FLOW

A lot of the things that have had the greatest impact on me are seeing how people rise in crisis. I saw this bear out in the Covid-19 pandemic, where people came together despite tremendous adversity to support those in need, those who were isolated, and those who were suffering. However, responding to large calamities, such as pandemics, natural disasters, or even human-made catastrophes takes tremendous amounts of energy. It became clear in the latter stages of the lockdown the level of effort required to keep the country running in conditions of shutdown and uncertainty was unsustainable.

When stripped down to essentials, when we see people in need, we are able, perhaps more able, to turn on the serve and support mindset. To be human. To step back from judgement and to begin with "how can I help?" How might we muster this most beautiful human spirit irrelevant of circumstance? How might we view our very selves as both enough, and capable of more at the same time? As much as we want to progress, want to thrive during periods of uncertainty, we have to do so in a way fuelled with inspiration and hope. By unlocking our inner flow, our best self we can continually adapt on a perpetual basis.

TO ACHIEVE THIS, WE HAVE TO RELEASE OURSELVES FROM JUDGEMENT.

We have to give ourselves permission to take a breath, to rest, and perhaps even to be a little selfish. We each must move **our own version of forward**. If we remember the example of the American football players, we can catch the ball only if we're running, but it is unnecessary that we all run at exactly the same pace, only that we're all moving and on the same playing field.

We live in a world full of great stories, amazing achievements, and truly superhuman successes. One can become heavy, down, and melancholy if seeing and reading of these phenomenal feats of success we allow the dark side of comparison to whisper in our ear: all those who have achieved success faster, younger, and easier than you— raised funds, accelerated their careers, and gained more media coverage, worked with a dream list of people and brands. I have often found the secret sauce is gratitude, to evoke a state of joy in humanity as one. To expand mentally with the notion of our collective capacity. To wonder, smile, and bask in the glow of shared experience. The very nature of learning about success and stories should expand our belief in the possible.

I recall the impact from watching the Netflix documentary *14 Peaks - Nothing Is Impossible*, the story of a fearless Nepali mountaineer Nimsdai Purja MBE who embarks on a seemingly unthinkable quest to summit all fourteen of the world's 8,000-metre peaks in seven months. A challenge fraught with surprises, obstacles, and an endless story of adaption, grit, resilience, and a profoundly positive mindset. When everyone was telling him the project could not be done, he named the endeavour "Project Possible". To put this into context, before Nims, the record for climbing all 14 peaks stood at eight years! To even conceive this could be achieved in seven months was beyond wild. The former UK Special Forces Operator had spent his life developing the skills and mindset to allow focus and decision-making under pressure in the most challenging of environments. His hashtag #allwaysalittlehigher enabled me to reflect not on his abilities in relation or judgement to mine, but on his principles and mindset—gaining energy from his story of overcoming the odds, in always finding a way, in his imagination and the relentless pursuit of his goals.

Whether it is a crisis or a dream which awakens the spirit inside, the precise call to our best self matters not. What counts is that we find the courage to try, to know our inner flow is already part of us. Perhaps the hardest comparison and judgement is the one we serve on ourselves. To know you are enough. To know you can be more. And that both are true simultaneously. We endeavour to move in rhythm and flow, and master when to be compassionate, humane, and forgiving, and when to be tough, honest and #allwaysalittlehigher. As my coach, Dan Sullivan says "all progress starts with telling the truth."

EXERCISE 12:

WHO INSPIRES YOU?

They could be someone famous or someone close to you.

....

....

WHY DO THEY INSPIRE YOU AND WHAT CAN YOU LEARN FROM THEM?

Don't compare your achievements with theirs. Instead, focus on how their achievements might inspire, fuel, and facilitate yours!

....

....

....

....

SUMMARY FOR PART 3

→ ADAPTABILITY IS NOT A SOLO JOURNEY, BUT SOMETHING WHICH INVOLVES OUR TEAMS, COLLABORATORS, AND COMMUNITIES

→ IT'S ONLY BY LEVERAGING ALL THREE OF OUR DIMENSIONS WE CAN ACHIEVE A BREAKTHROUGH AND UNLOCK OUR ADAPTABILITY POTENTIAL

→ THE POWER OF FRAMING. ALL SUCCESSES BELONG TO ALL OF US. WE ARE A SPECIES AND THUS ONE PERSON'S INNOVATION IS ALL OF OUR GAIN

→ COMMUNITIES ARE SO POWERFUL THEY MULTIPLY EVERYTHING, INCLUDING OUR "SHADOW"

→ RELEASE YOURSELF FROM JUDGEMENT—ALLOW YOURSELF SPACE TO REST

1 Psychologies Magazine; *Real Strength*; Capstone; 2017.
2 Diamandis, Peter; *Abundance: The Future Is Better Than You Think*; 2012.
3 Sullivan, Dan; Hardy, Dr Benjamin; *The Gap and the Gain*; 2021.

PART 4: RE-MODEL FROM REACT TO RESPOND

DATA OVERLOAD

It is often said that knowledge is power, but knowledge alone cannot change the world. We have to use that knowledge. In this chapter, I want to move from thinking to planning (which is the first stage of action!).

When facing uncertainty, one of our most basic and in-built reactions is to seek more knowledge, and more data, to help us combat our uncertainty–to move from the unknown to the known. It's a deeply ingrained pattern in us.

The greater the change, the more energy (and data) we require. "Hence, paradoxically, as we accumulate more data and increase our computing power, events become wilder and more unexpected."[1]

THE GREATER THE CHANGE REQUIRED
THE MORE ENERGY WE NEED

SUSTAINING OUR ENERGY & RESOURCES TO CONTINUALLY CHANGE BEGINS WITH RECOGNIZING THE DIFFERENT CAPACITIES WE HAVE. AND THE REPLENISHMENT TO CHANGE WITHOUT DESTRUCTION, BURNOUT OR BREAKDOWN.

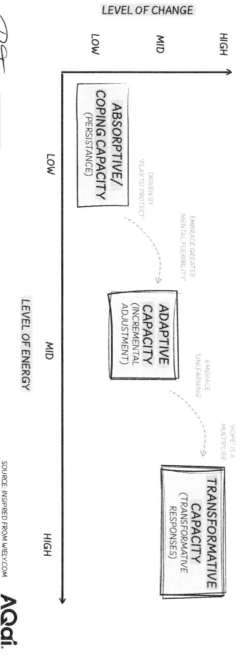

LEVEL OF CHANGE

HIGH

MID

LOW

LOW

ABSORPTIVE/ COPING CAPACITY
(PERSISTANCE)

DRIVEN BY 'PLAY TO PROTECT'

EMBRACE GREATER 'MENTAL FLEXIBILITY'

ADAPTIVE CAPACITY
(INCREMENTAL ADJUSTMENT)

EMBRACE 'UNLEARNING'

'HOPE' IS A MULTIPLIER

TRANSFORMATIVE CAPACITY
(TRANSFORMATIVE RESPONSES)

LOW

MID

HIGH

LEVEL OF ENERGY

THE AQ GUY

AQai

We can observe this process in even simple and day-to-day activities. If we want to travel somewhere, for example, we look up the route. If it's somewhere we don't visit frequently, we might also have concerns about traffic, so we'll look at the road reports or check Google Maps. We might even check the weather forecast. When we are in a relaxed and open mind frame, rather than an amygdala hijack, we use this data to create a plan. We choose to avoid certain roads. We map out our route. And we bring contingencies for the weather, such as an umbrella.

However, when we are in a fear state, and the amygdala is "in the driver's seat", no amount of data can actually help us. We can, in fact, suffer from "data overload" where we get stuck in a loop of consuming more and more information, believing that somehow it will solve our problem or alleviate our uncertainty, whereas actually each new piece of information only adds to our concern!

We need only look at Covid-19 as an easy example of this. During the height of lockdown, many of us were glued to our TV screens, watching the news, fed a daily meal of disaster, scary numbers, and new frightening research on the virus, and none of it helped us move from uncertainty to certainty, it only added to the fear! Likewise, in a business environment, with so much change happening, we can feel paralysed. We want to remove the paralysis by getting more information about this new "threat" we perceive, whether it's a "competitor", a disruption, an economic factor, or even an environmental problem. However, we have to recognise when to move from gathering data about a transformative event to creating a plan based on the information we have and trying to move forward.

There is a correlation between the size of the transformation event and the amount of data we think we require. In the previous example of bad weather and traffic on the roads, we need very little additional information to pivot our strategy. However, when a streaming service has rendered our brick-and-mortar store redundant, and our whole business model is overturned, we require much more information to deal with it! In fact, we might feel we require more information than perhaps possible for a human being to readily compute, which is why we have to begin moving forward, begin planning, and acting, even though we won't have all the answers at hand.

To do this, we need to find the right balance between **reacting** to problems and **responding** to them. This is because craving more data is *itself a reaction*, not a response. And worse, it can become an addiction too!

A *reaction* is automatic. When a bird swoops overhead, we duck. This is an innate, virtually genetic survival instinct that is in all of us. Sadly, these survival instincts—these automatic muscle-memory reactions—can play havoc with us as we try to navigate an ever-shifting exponential world. If every time we perceive ourselves to be threatened we either "duck" or "attack", we quickly alienate everyone around us.

There are several large corporations that recently posted massive losses because customers have become disillusioned by the way these organisations have treated smaller creators using their IP. Large corporations view suing others as protecting their interests, but when legal action starts to hurt people who are genuinely enthused about your product, people who are promoting your product for free (some coaches call these "super fans" for how they become walking advertisements of your product or service), it's a very ugly look indeed. The corporations who have instead *leveraged* the people enthused about their IP, on the other hand, are seeing massive wins.

This reminds me of a story once told to me by a friend of mine with an unusual background, given his current role; he was a school teacher for many years before becoming a coach, trainer, and entrepreneur (unusual, although no doubt that gives one a lot of insight into psychology and what is really motivating people from an early age). He was a drama teacher and was putting on a play in which he wanted to use the music of Paul Simon. Though he probably was being overly cautious, he called Paul Simon's agent and asked if they would be allowed to use the song in the school production. Simon's agent flatly refused and said they would sue the school if they went ahead and used the song anyway. My friend then called up the BeeGees' agent. The agent laughed at the very idea of a school teacher asking permission to use a song in a school play. The agent said that the BeeGees loved it when they heard about people using their material creatively and considered it a compliment. My friend concludes the story with a wry remark: "To my knowledge, the BeeGees have sold a fair few more records than Paul Simon." Indeed, they have sold approximately 213 million more! The generosity of spirit goes a long way. The BeeGees were not *threatened* by someone using their IP. They instead responded, recognising that all of this was simply a free promotion for them. To reiterate and emphasise my point here: the ability to be generous, rather than controlling and defensive, **comes from a responsive not a reactive place**. If we dwell in a reactive state, we won't be able to harness our giving and generous side.

In order to give a response, rather than succumbing to a reaction, we must harness "the pulse of adaptive behaviour". This "pulse" might be considered a deep breath, a pause. It is a moment where we step back rather than allowing the muscle memory of our in-built responses to take over.

FIVE POWERFUL LANGUAGE RE-FRAMES TO SHIFT FROM REACT TO RESPOND

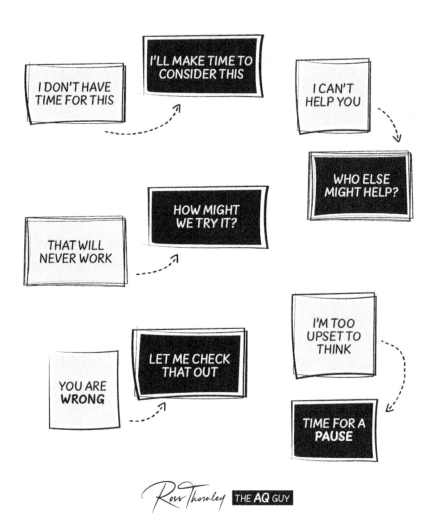

THE FOUR RS

Adaptive pulses are also about taking in the context of a situation. Had my friend been producing a play on the West End, then the response might have been different. It might have been perfectly reasonable for the BeeGees to have asked for a licensing fee for the use of their song. But the context was a school play.

Our society is, sadly, largely geared towards competition and avoidance of loss. This means we have a tendency to focus on short-term wins. As David Green observes: "Too many short-term performance goals focused on results and outputs can lead to an overly competitive environment where burn-out and one-upmanship pervade. Balancing these short-term goals with long-term goals focused on learning, mastery and the journey being taken will help to keep perspective and create an environment of greater collaboration, trust and sense of growth."[2]

I think of this as "zooming in and zooming out". In the corporate world, this tends to have the meaning of "big picture" thinking versus "detail". However, I think it is more useful to consider vantage points. What vantage points can we leverage to help us imaginatively? Rather than thirsting for data, can we move to a place of empathetic vision in which we see the so-called "problem" from an entirely different perspective?

When we're driving a car and we want to change gears, before we can shift into the next gear, we have to disengage the motion source, and go via "neutral". Going into neutral is in some ways quite scary because the car is in a state of undefined direction in neutral. And if we stay in neutral too long, we'll most certainly never get anywhere! However, without neutral, we cannot get anywhere else—forwards or backwards—we cannot shift gears.

Another term I use for this is "limbo". When we receive external stimuli we deem to be threatening, or when we enter the unknown, our minds and bodies, like a car, realise that they need to shift gear, and we need to enter a moment of neutral or limbo. Ken Wilber described this phenomenon in a fascinating analogy:

"For instance, if I come up behind you and yell 'Boo!' there will be a few seconds wherein you remain still, even though you have heard me yell, and during this very brief time **you might feel a type of passive or quiet alertness**, but this feeling shortly explodes into a sensation of mild shock (or something similar) accompanied with an onrush of thoughts and emotions… **In those few seconds of passive awareness, your Energy was beginning to mobilize but it was not yet experienced as shock or mild terror**–it was pure and without form, and only later did it disintegrate into thoughts and emotions of shock and fright."[3]

In other words, there is a moment before our reaction becomes manifest where we occupy a completely detached, objective, and unbiased vantage point whereby we can truly assess the correct response to a given stimulus. This limbo, then, is a realm of immense potential, especially when we consider that adaptability, "is the capacity to adjust one's thoughts and behaviours in order to effectively respond to uncertainty, new information, or changed circumstances."[4] By *leaning in* to this moment of limbo, by leaning into the pause, we can head off our reaction and instead craft a *response* with considered thought and action.

THE FOUR RS TO TRANSFORM SETBACKS INTO SPRINGBOARDS

To transition from "reaction" to "response" we can use my process of the Four Rs.

→ 1. RECOGNISE. THIS CORRELATES TO WHAT WE DISCUSSED EARLIER ABOUT SIMPLY OBSERVING, DECOUPLING FROM OUR EMOTIONS AND TAKING IN THE SITUATION WITHOUT FEELING THE NEED TO IDENTIFY WITH A SENSE OF FAILURE OR DESPAIR. THIS IS ENTERING "LIMBO" OR "NEUTRAL".

→ 2. REFLECT. ONCE WE HAVE TAKEN A MOMENT OF PAUSE TO "RECOGNISE" THE REALITY OF THE SITUATION, WE CAN MORE OBJECTIVELY "REFLECT" ON WHAT STEPS LED US TO THIS MOMENT OF SETBACK, WE CAN CONSIDER NEW INFORMATION, NOW IN AN ENHANCED COGNITIVE STATE.

→ 3. RE-IMAGINE. NOW, ARMED WITH VALUABLE KNOWLEDGE, WE CAN LOOK FORWARD INSTEAD OF BACK. WHAT NEW DOORS ARE AVAILABLE TO US? HOW CAN WE RE-IMAGINE OUR PARADIGM, OUR METHODOLOGY, OUR STRATEGY, OUR PROCESS, OUR WHATEVER— AND TURN THE SITUATION AROUND?

→ 4. RESPOND. NOW WE CAN TAKE DELIBERATE AND INTENTIONAL STEPS TOWARD NEW OPPORTUNITIES.

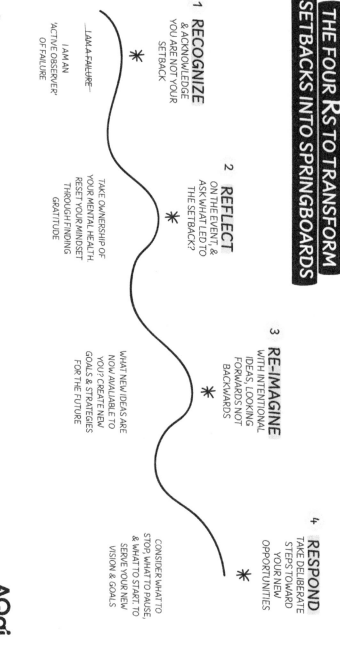

THE FOUR Rs TO TRANSFORM SETBACKS INTO SPRINGBOARDS

1 RECOGNIZE
& ACKNOWLEDGE
YOU ARE NOT YOUR
SETBACK

~~I AM A FAILURE~~

I AM AN
'ACTIVE OBSERVER'
OF FAILURE

2 REFLECT
ON THE EVENT, &
ASK WHAT LED TO
THE SETBACK?

TAKE OWNERSHIP OF
YOUR MENTAL HEALTH.
RESET YOUR MINDSET
THROUGH FINDING
GRATITUDE

3 RE-IMAGINE
WITH INTENTIONAL
IDEAS, LOOKING
FORWARDS NOT
BACKWARDS

WHAT NEW IDEAS ARE
NOW AVAILABLE TO
YOU? CREATE NEW
GOALS & STRATEGIES
FOR THE FUTURE

4 RESPOND
TAKE DELIBERATE
STEPS TOWARD
YOUR NEW
OPPORTUNITIES

CONSIDER WHAT TO
STOP, WHAT TO PAUSE,
& WHAT TO START. TO
SERVE YOUR NEW
VISION & GOALS

THE **AQ** GUY

AQai.

Of course, it is not easy to decouple from our emotions, nor is it easy to pause and observe events without becoming emotionally invested. By definition "limbo" is a scary place because it is neutral, because we do not see the familiar reminders and confirmations of our existing paradigms. This correlates with Mental Flexibility, or what Keats called "Negative Capability" and F. Scott Fitzgerald's praised as "the ability to hold two opposed ideas in mind at the same time and still retain the ability to function." It is in this "limbo" state, before *reaction*, that we can hold the multiple polarities in mind and decide consciously upon the right course. It is essential we learn to harness this power to enhance our adaptability intelligence.

Embracing alternative viewpoints correlates to step 2 of harnessing our AQ potential as leaders. Here is a handy summary that will show you where you may or may not be maximising this faculty:

SIGNS YOU MIGHT NOT BE MAXIMIZING YOUR ADAPTABILITY INTELLIGENCE

LANGUISHING IN A PLACE OF COMFORT OR FRUSTRATION, PARALYZES YOU FROM YOUR WORK AND LIFE. RECOGNIZE UNHEALTHY THOUGHTS, BEHAVIOURS AND PATTERNS, AND CREATE NEW, MORE PRODUCTIVE HABITS.

1   ONLY LISTENING TO ONE NEWS CHANNEL

2   SHALLOW BREATHING

3   LIMITING YOUR GOALS, BASED ON YOUR PAST

4   NOT CHALLENGING OTHERS, FOR FEAR OF CONFLICT

5   TOLERATING AN UNSUPPORTIVE ENVIRONMENT

Businesses tend to understand the world through two lenses: people who make what exists better, and people who imagine (and create) what doesn't exist. The paradox that we must embrace using Mental Flexibility is of course that we need to be doing both concurrently. The improvement of the old does not invalidate the creation of the new and vice-versa. However, we also have to recognise that existing within this paradox can be very draining. As we saw from the example by Ken Wilber, our responses *disperse* our mobilised energy. So, choosing a conscious, considered response costs us more energy than allowing muscle memory to take over. This is partly why muscle memory and automatic/involuntary reactions exist–as an efficiency. This is correlated with biology. If you want to make significant muscle gains, the worst thing you can do is the same routine every day. The muscles, tendons, and nervous system quickly acclimate to the familiar stresses and learn "shortcuts" that ease the load on the body. Therefore, the amount of benefit you gain from the training is a law of diminishing returns. Top trainers challenge their athletes with new and different exercises every single day so that their bodies cannot fall into this automatic and familiar routine. Our minds are the same!

VARIATION IS TO BE WELCOMED, NOT REJECTED AND FEARED.

In the world of work, we tend to imagine all processes and efforts as being regular, even, and balanced. The phrase "work/life" balance has permeated our everyday communications. As business owners, we are expected to increase profits by a predictable percentage each year. If we are not "growing" all the time, then surely we're dying? And so on. But the reality is that life moves in cycles and rhythms. We'll explore this in more detail later on, but for now, we can simply look at the "pulse of adaption".

The pulse of adaption is not just about the individual response and taking a pause before reacting to a situation. **It also operates at the organisational level.** As businesses, we must **build "pulses of adaption" into our work cycles.**

Rather than aiming for extreme levels of concentrated effort over extended periods of time, it is more realistic to attempt sprints of heightened effort that are then followed by a pulse, a pause, where we can assess what we've done, what the projections are, and where we might need to pivot. This manner of working might resemble a heartbeat. There is a rising peak of mental effort and concentration followed by a dip, a valley. This is the natural rhythm of existence. That is a business. That is life.

A PERFECTLY EVEN AND BALANCED FLATLINE IS, OF COURSE, DEATH!

By planning these moments of pause into your project lifecycle, and relinquishing the rigidity of "sticking to the plan", you will set yourself and your team up for success by becoming agile, adaptable, and *responsive* rather than "always-on" and *reactive*.

EXERCISE 13:

USING RECOGNISE, REFLECT, REIMAGINE, RESPOND, REVIEW A TIME IN YOUR LIFE WHEN YOU FEEL YOU RESPONDED WELL TO A SITUATION.

WHAT DID YOU RECOGNISE AND REFLECT ON?

....

....

....

....

....

....

HOW DID YOU RE-IMAGINE THE SITUATION?

....

....

....

....

....

AND WHAT COURSE OF ACTION DID YOU FINALLY DECIDE UPON?

....

....

....

THEN FLIP, WHEN DID YOU REACT TO A SITUATION IN WHICH YOU WOULD HAVE BENEFITED FROM FOLLOWING THE FOUR RS?

....

....

....

....

....

....

....

....

....

....

....

....

....

....

....

....

....

WRITE BOTH EXAMPLES DOWN AND SEE WHAT IT REVEALS, AND MAKE THE COMMITMENT TO LIVE MORE IN THE RESPONSE WORLD.

PARADOXICAL SYSTEMS THINKING

In order to further harness the adaptive pulse, we must examine our feedback loops more closely. As we mentioned, our ACE model of AQ is based on the input-process-output model of organisational psychology. This loop is used in virtually all experimentation and analytics in business. If we want to find out about employee turnover, we firstly gather data (usually over a period of time) and then input it into a process (a tool of measurement) and this gives us an output, usually a number or figure that tells us something meaningful. For example, "the employee turnover rate is 10% per annum." If we don't like the output, we then change something (offer greater flexibility, pay, or benefits like more perks or changing policies), and start the process again.

Solid though this model is, there is one slight issue with it—or rather, with *us*. That is the inherent cognitive bias that we explored in Part 1 of this book. We fixate on the negative. The very desire to measure employee turnover is an example of this! We devote massive effort and energy to measuring the employees that we are losing; we focus on that loss, rather than on those who have decided to stay, or people whom we might be looking to recruit!

A more dramatic example of this bias can be found in medieval history. When the Black Death swept across Europe in 1346, the doctors could not understand how to stop the disease. Many risked their lives dissecting patients who had been afflicted with the bubonic plague, only to expose themselves to the dreadful infection. Studying the Black Death surely puts our modern battle with Covid-19 into perspective. This is not to diminish the tragic impact of those who have lost their lives battling Covid-19, but the Black Death was a different calibre of beast, a monster that turned people into walking, putrefied corpses. It derives its name from how it turned the flesh black with gangrene. Eighty percent of those who contracted the bubonic plague died within merely eight days.

For years, the Black Death held Europe, Africa, and England in its sway. 50% of the entire population of Europe is thought to have been killed by it. The total number of lives worldwide claimed by the plague is thought to be 25 million people. If we consider the global population at the time, it is actually a wonder human civilisation was able to continue after such catastrophic losses.

How did they stop it?

There are a number of factors, of course: quarantines, the Great Fire of London which decimated the insect and rat population that were spreading the disease, and many other elements, but the answer as to how the cause of the disease was established and how it was "cured", is that they started to look at the people who weren't getting the plague. Their focus shifted from examining those succumbing to the illness to those who seemed naturally immune. What were these resilient people doing differently? How were they able to survive exposure to the illness? Essentially, the deciding factor was the diet. Those who were immune to the Black Death—or else survived having it—ate significantly more fruit and vegetables than those who'd died from it. In the latter stages of the Black Death, these immunised individuals were used for digging plague-pits and distributing alms and food because they were invulnerable to the plague.

As we can see, shifting our focus from the negative to the positive can provide us with solutions. By overcoming our inherent negative bias, we can begin to see the bigger picture. If we apply this logic to the employee turnover example: rather than measuring what we lose, why not measure what we have? What are we doing *right* that makes people stay? Once we have that data, then perhaps we can then do more of it! In business coaching lingo this is referred to as strength-finding. Rather than trying to address weaknesses, we capitalise on organisational strengths.

Of course, having said this, it is important to acknowledge the negative. I am not suggesting we blind ourselves to the reality of a situation. If your employee turnover is extremely high, then this is telling you something important and valuable, and perhaps drastic change is needed. However, in general, we have to consider more deeply the natural over-weighting of the negative and allowing it to overwhelm our thoughts and warp our strategies.

Simple though this technique is, for many years now **I START EVERY BUSINESS MEETING WITH A GRATITUDE FOCUS.** We begin with a positive note. Repeating this makes it a habit. By establishing this habit, we begin to erode the stranglehold that our cognitive bias has over our way of thinking.

INITIALLY, WE HAVE TO "OVER-WEIGHT" THE POSITIVE IN ORDER TO READJUST THE BALANCE SCALES OF OUR PSYCHE.

We live in a world of paradoxes, one where the duality of seemingly opposing thoughts and concepts can exist at the same time. Finding a place of peace in this poetic dance in the "in between" is a crucial step in building our adaptability intelligence, to reframing from a fight, from friction, and from one-must-prevail to harmony, abundance, and co-existence. To create this mental space, we must practise the expansion of our neutral state, a space absent of judgement. A space to breathe, to pause. A space to evaluate, before the considered flow into direction and decision. Be confident that there are many routes to any given outcome, so relax, there are no "wrong" moves. They all lead to progress, progress in learning, progress in the expansion of the mind, and in our life experience.

MAKING PEACE WITH PARADOXICAL THINKING

CREATING SPACE FOR MENTAL FLEXIBILITY TO ENHANCE YOUR ADAPTABILITY INTELLIGENCE

IT IS POSSIBLE TO BE...

GIVING
& SET BOUNDARIES

VULNERABLE
& SECURE

EXTROVERT
& ALONE

PERSEVERE
& LET GO

FAIL
& SUCCEED

HOPEFUL &
TRAUMATIZED

CONFIDENT
& QUESTIONING

INTROVERT
& REACH OUT

FEARFUL
& HOPEFUL

IRRELEVANT
& RELEVANT

 THE **AQ** GUY

EXERCISE 14:

LIST THREE THINGS YOU ARE GRATEFUL FOR AND WHY YOU ARE GRATEFUL FOR THEM.

Some people find it helpful to do this at the beginning or end of each day.

1. ....

....

....

2. ....

....

....

3. ....

....

....

NEXT, SEE IF YOU CAN FIND SIX PARADOXES THAT YOU ARE LIVING IN YOUR OWN LIFE. WRITE THEM DOWN.

Think about how this affects your thinking. And consider celebrating the duality of your life, one which can still flow in harmony, without the need for singular in all corners of our being.

....

....

RE-MODEL TO ROLE-MODEL

I have mentioned many times the accelerating pace of our world. We have now discussed duality and the importance of feedback loops. There is a temptation, faced with such rapid change, to think that the solution is to increase the speed of everything we're doing. We must get our products out faster. We must process orders quicker. We must provide more rapid delivery and service to customers.

You will be glad to learn that this is not necessarily the answer. It is a very literal and linear interpretation of the challenge at hand.

In American football, the ball seems to travel so fast the eye can barely keep up with it. Sitting in the stadium, watching as part of the audience, the speed is simply incredible. How can somebody *possibly* move fast enough to catch that? Yet players do, over and over again. It's no fluke. They do it all the time.

The secret, of course, is not just training, although that is undoubtedly important. It's a matter of *perspective*. Sitting stationary in the audience, the ball seems to move at lightning speed. The players on the pitch, however, are not stationary. They are moving. Some of them are running at over twenty miles per hour (albeit over short distances)! When you are moving at that kind of speed, the ball, relative to you, is not moving that fast at all. This means you have the time to see it and to catch it.

The key, then, is not to "speed up" our processes in the traditional sense, it's rather to keep moving. And the great news is that in reading this book, you're already in motion! This is the beginning. By opening your mind to the nature of adaptability, you're beginning to run on the pitch, and you're more ready than you were before to catch the ball.

When observing the success or failure of businesses over the long term, a study (cited by Napoleon Hill in *Think And Grow Rich*) revealed that the most important factor in a business's success was not whether its leaders made the right or wrong decisions at major junctures. Rather, it was that they made *a* decision. Failure came from either refusing to make a decision (we don't have to worry about x or y change, we're too big, for example,) or taking too long to make one (delaying in order to acquire more data). This is quite a startling revelation, and truly reveals the wisdom of the old proverb "Perfection is the enemy of progress."

By liberating ourselves from the colossal pressure of making the right or wrong decision as business leaders, and instead simply focusing on making *a* decision with the knowledge we have available, we can claim a sense of peace, and pace. True paradoxical systems thinking. As the philosopher, Alan Watts observed: "People experience a lot of anxiety over making a decision. We're always worrying, did I think this over long enough? Did I take enough data into consideration? But if you think it through you find that you never could take enough data into consideration. The data for a decision in any given situation *is infinite."*

The peace we obtain from owning our decisions is not some kind of mystical mumbo-jumbo but a real and lived experience. Rather than feeling oppressed by the need to make the "right" choice, we simply make choices freely. After all, we make decisions all the time without even being consciously aware of them. And even when we refuse to decide ("I'll do that later") that, *itself* is a decision!

In doing this, we become accountable for our decisions but not burdened by them. Combining this with remodelling our approach from *reactive* to *responsive* (using the Four Rs) is utterly transformational. We make progress toward the highest version of ourselves. The version of ourselves that is **of most service to others**. Rather than reacting to people's questions, we respond and answer them. Rather than agonising over decisions, we make them cleanly whilst accepting they may not produce the desired result; there is no blame here, only ownership. How often do leaders ask their employees to "take ownership" of their roles and responsibilities? We must likewise do the same. This allows us to become true role models for those in our communities.

On the subject of role-modelling it's worth returning to the example of the generosity of the BeeGees. We all have qualities within us that are of great benefit or inspiration to others: generosity, empathy, compassion, thoughtfulness, as well as what might be considered more directive leadership qualities, such as intelligence, insight, focus, etcetera etcetera. However, we'll only be able to let the light of these qualities shine if we move from reaction to response. Reactions never put others first because they don't consider context. Therefore, to truly become role-models, we must harness our ability to step back, consider, and respond.

EXERCISE 15:

WHO DO YOU WANT TO BE A ROLE MODEL FOR?

Write down a list of people. These could be family members, friends, employees, clients, colleagues, partners, or anybody who is within your sphere of influence.

....

....

....

....

....

WHAT IS ONE POSITIVE IMPACT YOU'D LIKE TO HAVE ON THEM?

Note: this doesn't necessarily mean changing who they are, this is never something we should aim to do—instead consider what you would like them to see in you!

....

....

....

....

....

....

SUMMARY FOR PART 4

→ REMODEL FROM REACTING TO RESPONDING

→ THE GREATER THE CHANGE, THE MORE ENERGY (AND DATA) WE BELIEVE WE REQUIRE

→ WE CAN HARNESS THE "NEUTRAL" OR "LIMBO" SPACE BEFORE REACTION TO CRAFT OUR RESPONSE, WITH PAUSE AND BREATH

→ SHIFTING OUR FOCUS FROM THE NEGATIVE TO THE POSITIVE CAN PREPARE AND PROVIDE US WITH SOLUTIONS

→ THE MOST IMPORTANT FACTOR IN A BUSINESS'S SUCCESS WAS NOT WHETHER ITS LEADERS MADE THE RIGHT OR WRONG DECISIONS AT MAJOR JUNCTURES. RATHER, IT WAS THAT THEY MADE **A** DECISION

1 Harai, Yuval Noah; *Homo Deus*; Harvill Secker; 2015.
2 David Green, The Age of Wellbeing, 2020
3 Wilber, Ken; *The Spectrum of Consciousness*; Quest Books; 1977. p310.
4 Martin, Nejad, Colmar, & Liem, 2013

PART 5: COMBATING OVERWHELM

ADAPTIVE CYCLES

E verything moves in cycles. Despite the evidence of this all around us—in the natural world, in our own professional and personal life cycles—businesses and organisations have a tendency to ignore this fact, seeking instead the Holy Grail of continual, predictable growth. When we unlearn this misleading societal expectation and reconnect with our environment, with the cycles, we can begin to harness our AQ potential.

ADAPTABILITY IS ITSELF A CONTINUAL CYCLE.

We tend to think of adaptability like we do employee engagement—like a badge. For example, we know we have to engage employees, so once a year we send out a company-wide Gallup survey for feedback. A little green checkbox is ticked. Job done! However, those who have more deeply explored the realm of employee engagement know that real engagement comes from a *continual, vigilant process*. Adaptability is similar in this regard. We do not "become" adaptable at any point, in one sense, as this would defeat the very nature of adaptability! Just as at no point can we say "employee engagement is complete" because to do so would be to say we are no longer listening to our employees!

Instead, adaptability is a cycle we engage in on an ongoing basis. If we understand the cycle more fully we can harness it to grow our adaptive muscles.

So, what is the cycle of adaptation? To help understand this I have created the "Four Worlds of Adaption" In short: Let's begin with a state of Thriving. Then this Thriving must inevitably Collapse. After Collapse, we must Survive. From Survival, we then Grow once more. And finally, having Grown, we Thrive again. This continual sequence plays out on both a small and large scale every day of our lives.

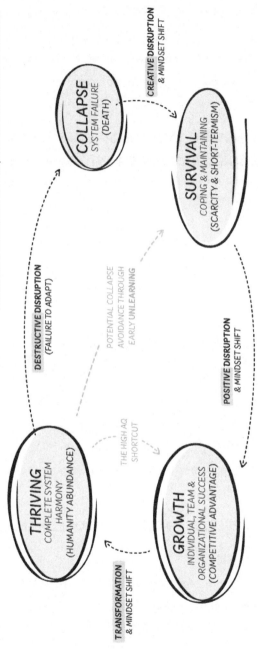

THE FOUR WORLDS OF ADAPTATION

THE CONTINUAL CYCLES OF CHANGE, THROUGH CREATION AND COLLAPSE

COLLAPSE
SYSTEM FAILURE
(DEATH)

SURVIVAL
COPING & MAINTAINING
(SCARCITY & SHORT-TERMISM)

THRIVING
COMPLETE SYSTEM
HARMONY
(HUMANITY ABUNDANCE)

GROWTH
INDIVIDUAL, TEAM &
ORGANIZATIONAL SUCCESS
(COMPETITIVE ADVANTAGE)

CREATIVE DISRUPTION
& MINDSET SHIFT

DESTRUCTIVE DISRUPTION
(FAILURE TO ADAPT)

POTENTIAL COLLAPSE
AVOIDANCE THROUGH
EARLY UNLEARNING

POSITIVE DISRUPTION
& MINDSET SHIFT

THE HIGH AQ
SHORTCUT

TRANSFORMATION
& MINDSET SHIFT

AQai.

THE AQ GUY

COPYRIGHT ADAPTAI LTD. | AQ® AND AQAI® ARE REGISTERED TRADEMARKS OF ADAPTAI LTD. | WWW.AQAI.IO

When we understand the cycle, we can begin to locate ourselves on the journey. Note that our position on the wheel is contextual and not all-encompassing. For example, our career might well be in the Thriving stage, but our relationship with our partner may have just Collapsed.

UNDERSTANDING THE CYCLE MEANS WE CAN DOCUMENT OUR EXPERIENCE, GIVING US AN INSIGHT INTO WHAT THE FUTURE MIGHT HOLD.

This isn't prophecy, of course, nor should we become fatalistic, but by mapping our position we can therefore project outcomes more realistically and reasonably than the "growth" graph we have come to know so well.

Furthermore, we can also avoid devastating losses.

For example, it might be that we do not need to *literally* Collapse in order to restart the cycle. It might be that we can perceive the natural order of things, that the period of Thriving is coming to an end, and instead willingly and intentionally—on our own terms—decide to fold and begin anew.

THIS ALSO CORRELATES TO FEEDBACK LOOPS—AND UNLEARNING.

One advantage of rapid feedback loops, in many ways, is to "shortcut" the cycle. By this, I mean the insights leveraged from a rapid experiment can allow us to sidestep Collapses and propel future endeavours more rapidly through the

Survival and Growth stages to Thriving. We do this by setting up an experiment in a test environment, so that rather than hard-committing to a new idea or proposition, we instead take the opportunity to explore it in an enclosed space (where Collapse doesn't mean Death!). In a test environment we might move from Survival through to Growth and then on to Thriving as normal, but rather than Collapsing, **we instead obtain information from this process** so that we can rapidly re-iterate the idea and improve it; this might, for example, take us from Thriving back to Growth, cutting out Collapse and Survival altogether because we are hitting the ground running.

I normally conduct these feedback loops in concentrated sprints to move through the adaptive cycle rapidly—perhaps in a few weeks or even a day. We might also find the shortcut hacks are able to help us avoid complete collapse, and limit the collapse to a specific area, say, a single product, task, or service, and not a whole company, job, or team.

Learning by doing is, of course, hard to beat. If you have ever had the experience of trying to learn a new board game, inevitably there comes a moment when you've read the rulebook three times through and it still seems like gobbledygook. After half an hour of exasperation, someone finally says, "Let's just try and play it," and invariably the game starts to make sense once the pieces are actually on the table and moving around. Sometimes no amount of theory can equal the act of putting ourselves in the action. And in our age of light-speed change, we *have to* learn by doing to a degree, because many of the things we need to do have never been done before, therefore there are no instruction manuals or rulebooks to read through!

However, we also have to honestly assess whether we are ready for the cycle. What will "Collapse" mean if we fail? If it means bankruptcy and death, perhaps we need to harness wargames, virtual reality, and other test environments first to simulate the cycle before we step into the cyclone of reality. Can we take a small experimental step to explore adaptability before we take the plunge of remodelling our whole business?

One tendency I've noticed in many struggling entrepreneurs and businesses is the propensity to linger. Too long in *any* phase (even Thriving!) can become corrosive. We might think this is impossible, but we only need to look at some of the former Forbes 500 supergiants who are no longer with us to see the principle illustrated. If we never enter pockets of "Collapse" then our ideas are never being challenged, which leads to stagnation and an inability to adapt and innovate in our approach. Likewise, if we take too long to dig ourselves out of a Collapse, our business may never get going again. We must recognise the value and importance of each phase without judgement—hard though that is! The collapse has its utility and purpose, as a radical driver of creation and innovation, and we must welcome it with open arms when it comes because it is going to lead us to new ideas and new potential.

EXERCISE 16:

It's time to map out your position in the adaptability cycle. Again, divide your life into three sections: work, relationships, and self.

SO, AT WHAT PHASE IS YOUR CAREER?

....

....

....

....

AT WHAT PHASE ARE YOUR RELATIONSHIPS?

....

....

....

AT WHAT PHASE IS YOUR PERSONAL DEVELOPMENT?

....

....

....

Even if some areas of your life are in a state of Collapse, take confidence from the fact that soon the cycle will shift and you will move to the next phase!

WHAT ONE ACT, WHAT ONE THING COULD YOU DO TODAY, TO HELP YOU MOVE FORWARD THROUGH THE CYCLE?

Check-out the shortcuts too!

....

....

....

....

....

CHOOSE WHO DRIVES

We have spoken at length about the challenge of the amygdala hijack, this biological process by which our reptilian brain tries to take control of the organism and govern our responses (or perhaps we should say "reactions"!). What we need, then, is *deliberate adaption*. This is a concept we'll return to and build on, but for now, I just want to outline what "deliberate adaption" is and how it can help us on our adaptability journey. Perhaps the best analogy I can give to understand the concept is the question of who is in the driving seat: Excitement or Fear.

It might be tempting for us to then think we want Excitement to be in the driver's seat all the time, and we need to "get rid of" Fear, and of course, Fear, as we've shown, is deleterious to cognitive function. However, we can't remove Fear—not without risking serious brain damage! And furthermore, Fear has its purpose. The negative aspects of life exist for a reason and are equally as valid and useful as the positive. For example, **we feel pain because pain preserves us from damage.** If we put our hand in the fire, it hurts us, so we withdraw our hand and thus save the skin from being burned. Likewise Fear is there to help us get out of situations where "the organism" might come to significant harm or even death. Fear can be a very powerful motivator. In fact, it might be one of the biggest. A man who has never run 5 kilometres in his life might run them to escape a hungry lion!

Therefore, **WE SHOULD NOT BE TRYING TO ESCAPE OR REMOVE THE FEAR RESPONSE BUT RATHER LEVERAGE IT BY INTENTIONALLY DECIDING WHO IS IN THE DRIVER'S SEAT.**

This is *deliberate adaption.*

It's deliberate because we choose. Some days we might need Excitement to get us through. The Excitement we feel about a project, a goal, or an imaginative dream might fuel us with the energy to manifest this as reality. However, on other days, imminent danger—financial hardship or collapse, a change in our environment—might be what we lean into to harness our deeper resourcefulness. Several colleagues of mine have left their jobs before they have secured a place at the next company. This might sound like an insane risk to some people, but the Fear of not having certain work lined up motivates them to push harder to find something they truly want, as well as giving them that killer edge in interviews. It's a common idiom that some people need a fire lit beneath them to start climbing the rope. In terms of AQ-Character we often look at this as Motivation Style. For some, moving away from disaster is a stronger motivator than moving towards some utopian dream. Once we know ourselves, we can harness this for our benefit **rather than being controlled by our biological reactions**. We *choose* to put Fear in the driver's seat because Fear will put the pedal to the metal in order to escape that tsunami rushing in!

To understand this *deliberate adaption* more clearly, and begin to exercise it, we can look at this three-stage process:

→ **1. RECOGNISE THE NEED (CONTEXT)**

→ **2. UNDERSTAND WHAT IS REQUIRED (ENVISAGE)**

→ **3. ACT (EMBRACE LEARNING BY DOING)**

CONTEXT

As mentioned earlier, different aspects of our lives sit at different stages of the adaption lifecycle. We, therefore, have to be very careful in identifying where we stand when it comes to deliberate adaption.

THIS IS SAYING NOTHING OF THE SPECIFIC AND UNIQUE CONTEXT OF EACH MOMENT-TO-MOMENT SITUATION OR CHALLENGE, THE ENVIRONMENT WE INHABIT, AND OUR PERSONAL AQ MAKEUP!

Tapping into our abilities as observers will be essential here. Rather than feeling tied up in the challenge, we have to step back, engage our "neutral", and simply perceive that it *is*. We can then determine where we are in the lifecycle—honestly and without bias.

ENVISAGE

It is one thing to identify a problem or challenge and how it has come about, but another to see the solution. In fact, my coach, Dan Sullivan, speaks of them as "all obstacles are the raw material for achieving your goals". This is why this stage is termed "envisage".

IT REQUIRES AN IMAGINATIVE LEAP FROM US TO SEE HOW WE MIGHT RESOLVE THE ISSUE OR "GET TO THE NEXT STAGE".

So, from observation, we do not immediately leap into action (that would be a *reaction*), we instead visualise the possibilities but retain this detachment to the situation and even its outcome. This allows us to run scenarios and strategies, and contemplate possibilities we might otherwise dismiss or throw out.

ACT

Now we have envisaged a multitude of solutions, we can decide, act on, and implement. This is, at last, where we can fully engage in *learning by doing*. It's therefore important even at this stage we retain an open-mindedness about what we do because it might be that in the doing, we discover some unforeseen opportunity (or even further obstacle). In other words, even the act of doing is a learning experience which allows us to gather information. This is all part of *deliberate adaption*. We don't do anything on automatic pilot, but rather everything becomes full of intent.

To take *deliberate adaption* one stage further, we can also become masters of our emotions. In the words of psychology professor Lisa Feldman Barrett, "We have misunderstood the nature of emotion for a very long time." Many of us believe emotions, including fear, happen to us, but the reality is quite different.

She outlines her findings in her TedTalk: "I have studied emotions as a scientist for the past 25 years and in my lab, we have probed human faces by measuring electrical signals that cause your facial muscles to contract to make facial expressions. We have scrutinised the human body and emotions. We have analysed hundreds of physiology studies involving 1000s of test subjects. We've scanned hundreds of brains and examined every brain imaging study on emotion that has been published in the past 20 years. And the results of all of this research are overwhelmingly consistent. It may feel to you like your emotions are hardwired and they just trigger and happen to you. **But they don't.**"

She goes on to explain that emotions are rooted in "predictions". In other words, our brains scan through past experiences and try to make sense of what we are seeing—our brains look for similar experiences or knowledge—and then give us a prediction or "guess" response. The truly mind-bending thing about this, however, is that we have far more control over our "guesses" or emotional responses than we think.

Barrett explains that our emotional responses are often comprised of very similar and simple physical and chemical components. For example, if we walk past a bakery and smell delicious cookies, our brain tells us that we're hungry, often by making our stomach rumble or "churn"! However, if we are waiting in a hospital waiting room, we might experience the same stomach-churning sensation, only we interpret it very differently. "Same physical sensations, same churning stomach, different experience. And so the lesson here is that emotions **which seem to happen to you are actually made by you.**"

Lisa Feldman Barrett advocates liberating ourselves from slavery to our emotions ("You aren't at the mercy of your emotions") and instead embracing a path of *choice.*

"You are not at the mercy of mythical emotion circuits which are buried deep inside some ancient part of your brain. You have more control over your emotions than you think you do. I don't mean that you can just snap your fingers and, you know, change how you feel the way that you would change your clothes. But your brain is wired so that if you change the ingredients that your brain uses to make emotion, then you can transform your emotional life."[1]

By pausing, considering the **context, envisaging** a new outcome, and **acting,** we can begin to initiate this transformation of our emotional lives.

EXERCISE 17:

USING CONTEXT, ENVISAGE, AND ACT, EXPLORE ONE OBSTACLE TO YOUR BUSINESS

This could be technological disruption, economic downturn, political upheaval, a people challenge, or simply a failed venture.

....

....

....

....

....

....

....

If you are employed, consider an obstacle to your current role.

....

....

....

....

....

....

....

....

HOW MIGHT YOU OVERCOME THIS USING THIS THREE-STEP PROCESS?

....

....

....

....

....

....

....

APPLY CURIOSITY

This is all very well, but what happens when the Fear takes hold very deeply, and we cannot seem to move them out of the driver's seat? The gold standard is, of course, to move towards deliberate adaption, but what can we do when we are in a situation we haven't chosen, and Fear is driving us at breakneck speed down some dangerous highway we don't want to be on?

THE ACTION WE MUST TAKE IN THIS SITUATION IS TO APPLY CURIOSITY.

We are most curious at five years old. In *The Curiosity Code*, Dr Diane Hamilton compares curiosity to a "spotlight" we are all born with and observes,

"Both animals and babies have spotlights, but infants and toddlers have the lens of their spotlights opened extremely wide. Their focus is all-consuming. They want to know about everything." When we are at this age, everything is new to us. We are astonished by even the most mundane facets of life and constantly ask the question "Why? Why? Why?"

Of course, as adults, we tend to use this question of "why" quite negatively. "Why is this happening to me?", often followed by "What did I do to deserve this?" If we can shift back to the child-like state of curiosity where we genuinely desire to seek new knowledge, then we can perhaps discover the sequence of events, the cause and effect, that led to an occurrence and understand what happened more deeply.

We can also harness curiosity as part of our adaptability training,

I run a weekly podcast on adaptability (surprise, surprise!). In each episode, I interview a new guest. One question I ask every guest is,

"WHEN WAS THE LAST TIME YOU DID SOMETHING FOR THE FIRST TIME? AND WHAT WAS IT?"

As an adult, this question can be surprisingly difficult for us to answer. It can be a very eye-opening moment when we realise how easily we have fallen into familiar patterns and routines. Remember the quote from Dryden, "We first make our habits, then our habits make us."

Most of my guests approach answering this question in one of two ways. The first is literal: they talk about something really "out there", a big experience they've never had before such as skydiving or hiking up a mountain. These can be very valuable experiences and can widen our perspective of not only what is out there but what we are capable of. However, not all of these experiences are highly accessible.

The second way I see this question answered is very relevant to this idea of curiosity. Usually, the guest talks about an experience they *have* done before, but with new eyes. As the French novelist, Marcel Proust beautifully put it,

"THE REAL VOYAGE OF DISCOVERY CONSISTS NOT IN SEEKING NEW LANDS BUT SEEING WITH NEW EYES."

This is much more accessible to all and is an interesting way of building our AQ muscles with a perspective shift so to speak. One exercise I recommend to clients is to visualise going for a usual walk or trip out, but doing a small section with their eyes closed (if you are blind, then you will have already exercised this adaptive muscle extensively, but perhaps there is a new way you could challenge yourself?). What strategies do we adopt to successfully and safely complete the walk? Might we walk slower? Do we hold onto something such as a railing or tree? Do we crawl on all fours? Do we seek the support and guidance of a friend? As you can see, something that—for most people—is easy and familiar suddenly becomes a great challenge and we have to move in radical and unusual ways in order to get to where we need to go. People recovering from serious illnesses often talk about the sense of wonderment and awe they feel making small gains back towards health. For example, the simple pleasure of walking to the corner shop can suddenly become a grand challenge one must bend will and intent toward after surgery or treatment. People who have been in these recovery situations understand how easily the known can become the unknown once again and that it is possible to re-learn, to re-skill, and metaphorically speaking to even go further than we ever went before getting ill. In fact, there are many stories of people who have recovered from serious health issues and ended up going on to run marathons and compete in high-level sports, which they never did before getting sick!

By challenging ourselves to complete an everyday challenge like this but with new parameters, we increase our tolerance of the unknown, of fear, and therefore, when we face the real thing, we are more prepared.

We tend to think of "pressure" as a bad thing.

We say, "I'm under pressure at work" or "That's a lot of pressure you're putting on me". However, the reality is we *need* a little bit of pressure. As mentioned before, the negative aspects of life all have their purpose. It's a cliche example, but when we apply pressure to ashes, we get diamonds! So, we should welcome pressure into our lives as a necessary catalyst for growth and transformation. The trick is having the ability to channel the pressure, to allow it to *flow through* us. Harnessing the creative power, and mitigating the worst aspects of its destructive force.

Interwoven with this idea of helpful pressure is that of "pace". Because of the lightning-fast speed of our exponential world, as I mentioned before we tend to think we have to adapt fast. This can lead us to reckless decisions, such as quitting our jobs seemingly overnight. Remember the earlier example of the American Football player. From the audience, tracking the speed of the ball is nigh on impossible, let alone catching it. But on the ground, while running, things are different.

If we focus on putting one foot in front of the other, of beginning our adaptability journey, we'll soon find that we are running, and in fact what seemed so lightning fast, so impossible to track, is actually much more comprehensible. These deliberate adaptions and exercises in curiosity are ways we can begin to break into a jog. Though they may seem minutely small, it is amazing how a few small things gradually add up to produce quite an awesome change. As the Tao Te Ching observes, "The journey of a thousand miles begins with a single step." Even the greatest leap and transformative change can be doable from the build-up of incremental steps. Just 1% better each day has a radical and exponential compounding effect. As James Clear illustrates in his book Atomic Habits: "In the beginning, there is basically no difference between making a choice that is 1 percent better or 1 percent worse. (In other words, it won't impact you very much today.) But as time goes on, these small improvements or declines compound and you suddenly find a very big gap between people who make slightly better decisions on a daily basis and those who don't.

Here's the punchline:

If you get one percent better each day for one year, you'll end up thirty-seven times better by the time you're done.

THE POWER OF TINY GAINS

1% BETTER EVERY DAY $\quad 1.01^{365} = $ **37.78**

1% WORSE EVERY DAY $\quad 0.99^{365} = 0.03$

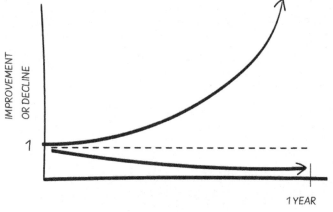

SOURCE: JAMESCLEAR.COM [2]

BREAKING OUT OF THE ECHO CHAMBER

Once we are up and running, we can begin to mix things up a little bit. Because if all our adaptions happen in "sameness"—the same culture, the same industry, the same field—then we miss out on what I call adjacent possibilities. We have to start somewhere, of course, but very quickly we will find ourselves approaching adaptability in the same way as any other corporate exercise. **THE IN-BUILT COPING MECHANISMS OF THE HUMAN BRAIN RUN ANTITHETICAL TO THE IDEA OF CONSTANT CHANGE.**

Therefore, if, for example, we decide to adapt our thinking around one of our product offerings, we very soon simply do this on a regular basis (perhaps twice a year), not realising that in making this process routine we are no longer really thinking in a flexible and adaptable way.

Part of the reason for this is the comfort we experience in the echo chamber.

Much has been written already on the stultifying effect of the echo chamber and how modern social media algorithms sadly encourage it. It is ironic that in a vast interconnected online world we actually might seem to experience less diversity of opinion than someone in the 20th Century who regularly visited the local pub! It can be hard work to escape our echo chambers and we have to intentionally seek out challenging opinions. When writing this book, I actively read vast numbers of books and papers, with some intentionally advocating for positions I fundamentally disagreed with in order to challenge my views and see, truly, what the other side was saying and whether there was any validity there. Doing so led me to development in my thinking and overall understanding of AQ.

But whilst technology might exacerbate the echo chamber effect, it is certainly not the cause. If technology creates silos, it is because we have designed it to create silos! Technology reflects our intent, not the other way around.

THE ECHO CHAMBER EFFECT DERIVES FROM A HUMAN NEED FOR ALIGNMENT.

Simply put, we like to hear voices and words we understand and make sense to us. We don't like hearing things that don't make sense, that we don't understand, or that—even worse—directly challenge our beliefs! In many circumstances, this elicits the fear response because in the past hearing a sound, a word, or an idea we didn't understand might very well lead to death. This might sound extreme, particularly in relation to the last example, but one only needs to consider something every day we take for granted, such as eating food, to see what I mean.

Imagine you are a cave person living in a small community, and you have been living well for the last decade hunting and gathering, but suddenly you find that there is a food shortage. You don't know what to do about this food shortage. Suddenly, a cave-person you have not seen in many years comes to your cave and shows you a large fish. You have never seen this creature before in your life, but the other cave person says he found it on his travels, and he can get more fish like it, and that it is edible and delicious. The food shortage is solved!

Everyone is happy—that is, until a day later they realise the fish is poisonous. Many die before they can purge the toxicity out of their digestive system. In this context, eating fish is a new idea—and the idea directly leads to harm. Hence, we, as a species, are programmed from our earliest beginnings to view new ideas with suspicion. Now, it might seem obvious to us that eating food from a spurious source might be dangerous, but the example above is harkening back to a time when food was incredibly scarce and little was known about the world. If we translate this analogy into modern terms we see that many of the new, exponential fields opening up such as AI, biological augmentation, virtual reality, genetic manipulation, etc., are areas in which we know about as much as the average caveman did about exotic fish!

Obviously, not all new ideas are dangerous or likely to lead to "death". To continue the metaphor, the cave-person in the above example who suggested they eat the fish—provided they survived the ordeal—would likely be branded as someone with "bad ideas", someone who should not be trusted with future decisions. This is a shame as it might be the case their next idea was a valid and useful innovation (they might have been the literal inventor of the wheel)! I am being playful here, but it serves to illustrate how we can very quickly shut down suggestions or innovations based on past "losses" or negative experiences even when they have objective value. We have to break down these mental obstacles if we are to truly benefit from new inputs and not become isolated in an echo chamber that continually reinforces our current worldview. At the same time we remain aware there are genuine risks out there; this is going to challenge our Mental Flexibility!

To put this another way, we may not have to accept the fish blindly, **but we can offer to go with the other cave person to the source and investigate the fish for ourselves.** By doing so, we might perceive readily that the fish are toxic, and therefore make an informed decision not to eat them. Along the way, we're likely to have discovered a new opportunity.

When we undertake the journey to see the other person's viewpoint, opinion, or idea, we begin the process of **expansion and exploration**. This can open up new pathways and even more excitingly: new goals can emerge. Many explorers of the ancient world returned from their travels with a recalibrated purpose. In fact, my own perspective and mission in life adapted when I visited Africa to conduct research on behalf of the United Nations. Though in truth a mere toe-dip into the wider world beyond my Western experience, it opened my eyes to vast cultural differences, lifestyles, and creative endeavours I could not have imagined.

We must enter the unknown with a sense of **curiosity**. Only then can we see the opportunities a new landscape might hold.

EXERCISE 18:

Consider the various communities you are a part of, including social media and the online world.

ASK YOURSELF WHETHER YOU ARE SUFFERING FROM THE ECHO-CHAMBER EFFECT IN ANY OF THEM. WHERE MIGHT YOU SAFELY GO TO HEAR AN ALTERNATIVE VIEWPOINT?

....

....

....

....

COULD YOU CHALLENGE YOURSELF TO TRULY LISTEN TO OPPOSING VIEWPOINTS OF A DIFFERENT POLITICAL PARTY, TO PEOPLE WHO HOLD DIFFERING VIEWS OF TECHNOLOGY, OR TO HUMAN RIGHTS ISSUES?

The deeper your conviction and belief, the harder it is to "hear" the strange and opposing view.

....

....

....

....

THIS ISN'T HAPPENING TO YOU, IT'S HAPPENING FOR YOU

Yuval Noah Harai said that "Historians study the past not in order to repeat it, but in order to be liberated from it."[3] I'm inclined to agree. We can only transcend negative cycles by first understanding how they came about.

In relation to the cycle of adaption, this is more true than ever. By analysing our past cycles—the how, why, and what that caused our "Collapse"—we can move forward into a brighter future in which we are in control (we choose who is in the driver's seat). When done with intention (again, returning to this idea of *deliberate adaption*), Collapse is not true Collapse nor even failure **BUT A CHOICE TO RELEASE SOMETHING THAT IS NO LONGER SERVING. THROUGH THIS, WE TRANSFORM OUR "COLLAPSES" INTO A DELIBERATE UNLEARNING EXPERIENCE.**

When we harness our curiosity and turn our "defeats" into an Unlearning process by which we are constantly letting go of what doesn't serve and developing new things that do serve us and others, we become powerhouses of imaginative influence and abundance. Furthermore, we no longer fear the unknown—the words we don't understand or the views that challenge us—because we have obtained a degree of contentment or transcendence. We are in a state of flow, or eternal now, moving *with* the cycles rather than against them.

IN OTHER WORDS, WE DON'T LEARN ADAPTABILITY, WE BECOME IT.

EXERCISE 19:

WHAT IS ONE HABIT YOU WOULD LIKE TO RELEASE?

WRITE DOWN ONE SMALL HABIT THAT IS NO LONGER SERVING YOU, NO LONGER FIT FOR YOUR FUTURE SELF.

And consider how you might use what you have learned so far in the book to intentionally let it go.

....

....

....

....

....

WHAT WOULD IT TAKE TO RELEASE THAT HABIT AND "UNLEARN" IT?

....

....

....

....

....

....

....

SUMMARY FOR PART 5

→ ADAPTABILITY IS A CONTINUAL CYCLE

→ FEEDBACK LOOPS ALLOW US TO "SHORTCUT" THE CYCLE

→ WE CAN LEVERAGE FEAR WITH DELIBERATE ADAPTION TO AVOID "COLLAPSE"

→ CURIOSITY CAN HELP US HARNESS BETTER "GROWTH"

→ USE CURIOSITY TO TRANSFORM "COLLAPSES" INTO AN UNLEARNING EXPERIENCE

1 Barrett, Feldman Lisa; TedTalk, Jan 2018.
2 https://jamesclear.com/continuous-improvement
3 Harai, Yuval Noah; *Homo Deus*; Harvill Secker; 2015.

PART 6: RAPID FEEDBACK LOOPS

BECOME A LIFELONG LEARNER

We have lightly discussed rapid feedback loops, but it is worth devoting a little more time to them. We tend to think of rapid feedback loops as part of the corporate process, but they are also part of life's process. We are constantly in a process of evaluating what we have done and what we will do next. In fact, when we stop doing this, often that is when problems creep in. For example, you keep eating the same food even though the feedback from the food is that it's making you feel unwell and overweight. If we can embrace the adaptive cycle and engage in day-to-day rapid feedback loops we become lifelong learners who can avoid these stagnant pitfalls.

However, our society is not largely geared up for this mode of continual autodidacticism. We are mired in the traditions of academic institutions and "places" that we go to in order to "acquire" learning. But learning doesn't have to look like that. Learning can be a daily revolution.

In *Moonshot Thinking*[1], a powerful video about moonshots and one of my favourite inspirational talks, Astro Teller illustrates the challenge we face of breaking through the paradigms beautifully: "If you want cars to run at 50 miles per gallon: fine, you can retool your car a little bit. But if I tell you it has to run on a gallon of gas for 500 miles: you have to start over."

A moonshot is an idea so big that we don't actually know how we're going to achieve it at the outset. In other words, a moonshot isn't a moonshot if we know how to do it. As Yuval Noah Harai writes in *Homo Deus*, "History is often shaped by exaggerated hopes." To achieve a moonshot, we have to think more flexibly than ever. If we are too attached to the old ways of doing things, the familiar processes, we will never be able to create something radical and new or reinvent an old process. This concept reinforces the importance of continuous learning, continuous curiosity and openness to new ideas and discoveries while balancing this with Grit to see a long-standing goal through.

Astro Teller is himself an embodiment of Mental Flexibility. He holds a bachelor's and Masters's in the science of symbolic computation (from Stanford), and a PhD in artificial intelligence from Carnegie Mellon University. In 1997, he published his first science fiction novel, *Exegesis*, exploring the relationship between a researcher and a self-aware AI, Edgar. His second novel, *Among These Savage Thoughts*, is wildly different, exploring the inner world of an assassin in an imaginary mountain society. His last book is a non-fiction title, co-written with his wife Danielle, that deals with the "sacred cows" (a term for widely held assumptions and misinformation) about divorce, marriage, and love. It's easy to see the great diversity of his creative output. This is saying nothing of the 60 patents he holds for various software and hardware inventions.

Astro has been called the "**Captain of Moonshots**". From 2010 onwards, he has directed Google X, or what is now called simply X, a "moonshot factory". Some of his projects include Google Glass, Google Contact Lens, Google Driverless, and Project Loon (a subsidiary working on providing internet access to rural areas).

So, how does Astro Teller achieve this Mental Flexibility and open-mindedness to explore new creative avenues?

In his article *How Google X works*, published in Fortune in 2014, he described what a moonshot is and how to approach it: "The first one is that it's a huge problem. That sounds pretty obvious, but it's incredibly not obvious in fact. Then the second thing is that there has to be some kind of radical proposed solution. It should be a science fiction-sounding product or service. Obviously, whether it really sounds like it comes out of Asimov isn't important. What's important is that we be not treading the same ground that other people have tread before because thinking that we're going to be smarter or better resourced or work harder than people who've come before us is just not a good bet."

The solution should sound like "science fiction" because really this requires true flexibility to imagine and dream. We, as human beings, have such a powerful capacity to imagine. In fact, I believe we are moving from an information and knowledge economy into an imagination economy, where we will place the greatest value on those who are able to articulate the best questions, and dream new worlds for us—giving rise to the **contextualizers, the dreamers**, and most the ambitious. The power of dreams is precisely their ephemerality. We can become attached to them, but often we have to move on from them. When working on Project Loon, which had the ambitious aim of getting five billion people connected to the internet via high-altitude balloons, Astro said their thought process had to completely shift from "This is going to work" to "This is not going to work." He had to let go of wanting to succeed.

In fact, Project Loon became about attempting to *disprove* that it was possible to do it:

"HOW CAN WE DISCOVER WHY THIS WON'T WORK AS FAST AS POSSIBLE SO THAT WE CAN DISCARD THIS AND MOVE ON TO SOMETHING ELSE?"

It was only after a year of experimentation and testing that they "[started] to take this project really seriously." This goes to show that failure is not just an important part of the creative process, it is the creative process.

In 2016, Astro gave a TEDTalk where he highlighted the "critical importance of failure" to the creative process and pioneering new technology at Google.

In an article published by *Fast Company*, Astro highlights even more of the creative process. Google X has a Rapid Evaluation Team; "Rapid Eval" for short. Teller describes them as "polymaths" (someone with extraordinarily wide knowledge and learning), and their purpose is to vet ideas, essentially by doing everything they can to prototype them and then break them. This chimes with my own thoughts. In my book *Moonshot Innovation*, I describe the qualities of an exponential leader, one of which is becoming a BET (Broad Exponential Technologist). It is not about having one area of specific knowledge but a broader spectrum of awareness about what is out there, how it is being used, and where different technologies can intersect for common good.

To return to Rapid Eval: in many ways, the emphasis is on failure and rejection. Just as much importance is placed on rejecting ideas as on putting them through. This is an intriguing reversal. It makes me think that the creators at Google X, the ones responsible for submitting ideas to Rapid Eval, must have extraordinary Resilience as well as Mental Flexibility in order to be able to handle the rejection of their creative efforts.

Rich DeVaul, the head of Rapid Eval, says: "Why put off failing until tomorrow or next week if you can fail now?" Every failure is a chance to discover something new, an opportunity to learn, and brings us one step closer to changing the world.

Here is a game you can play to develop your moonshot thinking, inspired by "Moonshots in a Box".

FIND TEN BLANK CARDS AND MARK THEM AS 'PROBLEMS'.

Write down some of the world's biggest concerns: world hunger, poverty, inequality, war, bacterial resistance, and any issue that resonates with you. Using inspiration from the UN Global Goals is a good place to start.

NOW, TAKE TEN MORE CARDS AND MARK THEM AS 'TECHNOLOGIES'.

Write down any crazy sci-fi technology you can think of. It could be hoverboards, spaceships, or cloning, it doesn't have to be available to everyone now, let your imagination run riot.

Shuffle the problems and shuffle the technologies and then draw one of each. You now have to come up with a way to use that technology to solve the problem on the card.

WRITE DOWN YOUR SOLUTION IN 50 OR SO WORDS.

This is a great team exercise in creativity and mental flexibility.

Create without judgement to expand your horizons of seemingly impossible thinking.

THINK IN PRINCIPLES

We become very emotionally attached to the knowledge or methods that "got us here". **THIS IS BECAUSE WE INVEST TREMENDOUS ENERGY AND RESOURCES IN THE PROCESS OF ACQUIRING SAID KNOWLEDGE OR EXPERTISE,** and one reason why the process of unlearning or letting go of old/redundant information is so hard. It can truly feel like ripping out a part of ourselves. However, we must let go if we are to adapt and fulfil our dreams—our moonshots.

Imagine a staircase. You place one foot on the lowest step. This is symbolic of the knowledge you have acquired so far. You place your other foot on the next step up. Your current knowledge base got you to this second step. Congratulations! However, if you want to make it to the third and fourth and fifth steps— maybe even to the top of the staircase—*you have to take your foot off the first step.* If you think about it, it's literally *impossible* to climb any higher without first letting go! If we remain rooted to the first step, refusing to take our foot off it, then we can't get any higher. Sadly this is the case for many people who are too emotionally attached to a particular set of skills, knowledge base, or expertise.

Education—or at least traditional modes of education in the West—tends to be very focused on the end result. We memorise the answers to tests. Even in situations where we're asked to "show our workings", we are marked down if our workings are unconventional or don't conform to the normal procedure. In my view, we have placed excessive focus on the end result to the detriment of our development and growth and the continual learning experience. It's not all bad news, however, things are shifting, and new methodologies are beginning to emerge in pockets of the education system.

Of course, this is not to diminish the importance of outcomes in business. We want our efforts to produce tangible results. However, in an exponential world, the end result might well be a moving target!

ONE OF THE CORE PRINCIPLES OF SCIENCE IN GENERAL IS ENSURING THAT MEASURES ARE RELIABLE, AND THAT THE METHODS WE USE TO OBTAIN AN OUTPUT ARE VALID.

This can be of great service to us in a world where the goalposts are constantly shifting.

To illustrate with an example, if we invest everything in pursuing an outcome, let's say creating a product that provides X function (measuring real-time blood sugar for diabetics, without the need for a prick-test), only for a new piece of technology to emerge a few months later that completely invalidates and outmodes the need for the end function (a cure for diabetes), then all that investment and energy is going to feel like a huge waste of time.

HOWEVER, IF WE SHIFT OUR FOCUS TO CREATING VALID AND ROBUST METHODOLOGIES, THEN THESE ARE FAR LESS LIKELY TO GO OUT OF DATE.

The risk of a process that is valid and reliable becoming obsolete is far less. Therefore, if we improve our processes, the fundamental methods by which we create and contribute value to the world, then we are future-proofing our businesses. New products and technologies may emerge, but they will not likely displace our continual adaptation and innovation process. The Rapid Evaluation team at Google X is a prime example of this. The process is solid which facilitates the adaptive, explorative creation of new products, new moonshots, and new dreams.

I should add one caveat here: rapid experimentation and rapid feedback loops only work in an environment of "psychological safety". In other words, only if the culture of the workplace is one of openness, sharing, non-judgement, and complete transparency can this kind of system work. Adam Grant said, "It's not psychological safety if people can only voice what you want to hear. The goal is not to be comfortable. It's to create a climate where people can speak up without fear. Psychological safety begins with admitting our own mistakes and welcoming criticism from others." If a radical idea is laughed out of the room the first time we decide to share, then obviously one feels less likely to ever contribute a radical idea again.

THIS PLACES A GREATER EMPHASIS ON THE COMMUNITIES WE CURATE.

As leaders, we, therefore, have to cultivate this psychologically safe environment where "team support", "emotional health", and "company support" facilitate a level of playful wonder, joy and discovery. No bad idea, no wrong questions, and where our hypothesis can be as outlandish and large-scale as the imagination allows.

EXERCISE 21:

IS YOUR WORK CULTURE "PSYCHOLOGICALLY SAFE"?

Check the table opposite and see where your organisation falls on the continuum.

HOW TO SPOT ENVIRONMENTS WHICH SUPPORT HIGHLY ADAPTABLE BEHAVIOURS

 LOW ADAPTATION ENVIRONMENT

 HIGH ADAPTATION ENVIRONMENT

LOW ADAPTATION ENVIRONMENT	HIGH ADAPTATION ENVIRONMENT
• FEEL ISOLATED	• FEEL VALUED
• REGULARLY EXPERIENCE NEGATIVE EMOTIONS	• REGULARLY EXPERIENCE JOY & EXCITMENT
• SHARING NEW IDEAS IS RISKY	• SHARING NEW IDEAS IS CELEBRATED & REWARDED
• AVOID PROBLEMS	• BRING UP ISSUES WITHOUT JUDGEMENT
• HIDE MISTAKES	• OPENLY DISCUSS MISTAKES ACROSS WHOLE ORGANIZATION
• UNABLE TO FINISH TASKS	• ABLE TO FINISH TASKS

Ross Thornley THE **AQ** GUY

AQai.

THE MULTIPLIER OF COMMUNITIES

It was motivational speaker Jim Rohn who famously said: "You are the sum of the five people you spend the most time with." I believe this to an extent, but I think our environments, the way we spend our time, and the influence of technology, are going to change that paradigm.

Traditionally, a community is a group of like-minded people that come together for a shared purpose. The members of a community will likely share characteristics or values that unite them in their purpose. They may live in proximity, but with the emergence of our digitally connected world that is increasingly becoming a thing of the past. People can maintain fruitful connections with people all over the world via the Internet.

In terms of AQ, we consider whether the Environment helps or hinders adaption. Community is naturally one of the most important parts of our Environment. Previously, we've thought about community as the people we work with. However, in today's world, and certainly the world of the near future that will seem like science fiction to most, I think we have to also acknowledge that technology is itself a part of our community. What technology do we have access to in our Environment, and how does that affect our ability to be adaptable, to experiment, and to make breakthroughs? If I spend lots of time talking to Siri or Alexa or our very own artificially intelligent chatbot, Aida, how does that affect my adaptability? What about my employees? What technology are they interacting with on a regular basis? What platforms do we use to facilitate communication? Slack? Email? Or something else? We may indeed spend a significant proportion of our days with avatars and "AI beings" perhaps as our guide, our mentors, our coaches, or even future partners! How might this influence our environment?

Technology has already transformed the way we socially interact and build communities. Social media allows us to connect and keep up-to-date with thousands of people, more than we could without it. Of course, this is not necessarily all good, as social media also has negative aspects (social comparison leading to negative effects on mental health, false reality, and echo chambers of opinion). However, the reality is technology has changed the way we connect with people. Consider how apps have transformed dating. The majority of young people now use apps to meet their other halves. Sometimes this is casual, of course. But many find real long-term partners.

Technology has also transformed the way corporate teams are able to work together. It's easier than ever before to work remotely, and even globally, using Google Docs, Zoom, Slack, Skype and other such tools. Remote-desktop viewing means we can even control other devices. Teams no longer need to inhabit an office space from nine to five. They can work in more flexible and agile ways. All of this has happened in the last ten years and Covid-19 has wildly accelerated the process.

So, when we ask ourselves, who are the five people I spend the most time with and are they helping or hindering my adaptability? Might we need to include technology in that? Am I spending more time with Facebook, TikTok, or other apps? How is that changing the way I think, behave, and ultimately adapt?

I also like to think of the "five closest people" across five categories, because, although I am a firm believer that all aspects of our lives should connect to who we are, we are living in a more multifaceted world.

We might consider the five closest people in our:

→ **TEAM**

→ **OUR ORGANISATION AS A WHOLE**

→ **OUR SUPPLIERS**

→ **OUR INDUSTRY**

→ **OUR FAMILY**

→ **AND TECHNOLOGY ITSELF**

So, our Team is made up of the people we immediately work with. We probably spend the most time with these people, perhaps even on a daily basis. In a traditional organisational arrangement (and these are rapidly evaporating it must be said), this might well be people in the same department as us. Even though many now work remotely, and a startling number of people are choosing to be self-employed, it's likely we will still have teams that surround us and that we have regular contact with. An author friend of mine refers to his "team" of beta-readers, cover-designers, and editors!

Considering our Organisation as a whole, then: Who are the key people across the departments we work with? Do you regularly interact, say, with someone in Accounts, someone in HR, someone in Sales, and a senior manager? Are they the key people outside your team whom you have the most contact with? What do they bring to the table? How do they help your adaptability or hinder it?

Many people do not consider Suppliers to be relevant unless they are directly working in the type of industry that needs materials. However, we unknowingly work with suppliers all the time. Our Internet service providers, our social media platform providers, and our web developers—all our suppliers. Less directly, I regard the people who give us *learning tools* to take on new challenges as suppliers. They provide us with invisible resources that help us combat our problems. Technology like "miro" or "mural" allows us to collaborate in the virtual world, much like we used to with post-its and whiteboards. So this technology community multiplier in our environment has an unlocking and expansion benefit. Plus it gifts us a unique experience with the ability to harness asynchronous collaboration too.

Consider more broadly who *your* suppliers are. If you're running a coaching business, for example, then you might well have very few *physical* components to your business. You're not making products, you're selling your abilities and your knowledge. However, you still have suppliers, and these need to be cultivated, as they for sure influence your ability to adapt and deliver in new contexts.

→   *YOUR FIVE PEOPLE IN THE INDUSTRY SHOULD BE ROLE MODELS.*

→   *WHO ARE YOU LOOKING UP TO?*

→   *WHO ARE THE GAME-CHANGERS IN YOUR FIELD?*

→   *WHO IS INSPIRING YOU?*

If your industry experts are writing books and you're reading them, what effect is their input having on your adaptability? Is there anyone that you are spending lots of time following that, upon reflection, you feel might not be the best role model? Would you benefit from a shift in your focus from them to someone else? Also, how diverse is your selection? You may not have a choice about your Team or Organisational connections, but you have complete control over who you look up to in your industry. Are they all men? Do they all have the same background? The most commercially successful people are not necessarily the best role models, of course. Look to the people who are trying to do things differently. Go on, step outside the usual "echo chamber".

And finally, Technology. What are the five technologies that are influencing your industry, your organisation, and *you*? How much time do you spend with them and what is the effect of that? Do they trap you in the ways and methods of the past, or are they freeing you up to the potential of the future?

Technology is increasingly going to become a part of our lives, from our social interactions to our business ventures. It's time to open our arms and embrace it as part of our Community.

EXERCISE 22:

Complete the exercise outlined in the above segment:

WRITE DOWN THE FIVE PEOPLE YOU SPEND THE MOST TIME WITH

in your Team.

1. ....

2. ....

3. ....

4. ....

5. ....

---

in your Organisation.

1. ....
2. ....
3. ....
4. ....
5. ....

from your Suppliers.

1. ....
2. ....
3. ....
4. ....
5. ....

from your Industry.

1. ....
2. ....
3. ....
4. ....
5. ....

from your Family.

1. ....
2. ....
3. ....
4. ....
5. ....

in terms of Technology.

1. ....

2. ....

3. ....

4. ....

5. ....

Consider what their impact might be on you.

WHAT DOES THIS PROCESS REVEAL?

....

....

....

....

....

....

....

....

....

....

....

LEAVING NO ONE BEHIND

When we read about sub-dimensions of AQ such as Resilience and Grit, we might think we need to become more monomaniacal and focused—that we must pursue a North Star to the exclusion of all else. But, as we have seen, things are not that simple. We have to balance our Resilience and our Grit—the ability to resume action, and the determination to see things through—with an openness to unlearning and re-evaluating.

Society has built a construct, and in part convinced us, that abandoning an objective is a terrible and shameful failure. We all know the phrase "Oh, you didn't *stick with it*" when someone hears you decided not to pursue an activity to its so-called conclusion. Stick is the operative word in that sentence, however. When we linger too long we tend to get *stuck* in the wrong way.

If you played an instrument as a child but didn't carry on into adulthood, people often condemn you as not "staying the course". The reality is you may have stopped playing because you (a) didn't enjoy it and (b) it no longer served your ambitions. Though we can achieve much more than we ever dream, the reality is to achieve something we have to invest time in it and we only have a limited amount of time during a single day or lifetime no matter how efficiently we use it. Something has to give. The idea of the Renaissance Man was a noble one in the 17th Century but in the exponential world, we inhabit it might not be an achievable ambition, even if we were to live 200 years!

The Harvard Business Review sheds light on this in their article "The Dark Side of Resilience": "extreme resilience could drive people to become overly persistent with unattainable goals. Although we tend to celebrate individuals who aim high or dream big, it is usually more effective to adjust one's goals to more achievable levels, which means giving up on others. Indeed, scientific reviews[2] show that most people waste an enormous amount of time persisting with unrealistic goals, a phenomenon called the "false hope syndrome." Even when past behaviours clearly suggest that goals are unlikely to be attained, overconfidence and an unfounded degree of optimism can lead to people wasting energy on pointless tasks."[3]

I, therefore, want to give you permission to let go of your goals. I should say this with a heavy caveat that this is not an excuse or permission to stop trying at all, but rather giving you the opportunity to recognise—in a moment of truth and honesty—whether a goal is actually harming more than helping, does it still hold true the future vision of yourself? Some goals might not be possible for you where you currently stand, or worse they might be possible but at too high a cost. I know people who have tried to run marathons and quite literally come close to killing themselves in the process of training. It's an admirable goal to run the marathon, but there are many other ways to raise money for charity, gain a sense of self-achievement, and keep healthy. Indeed, there are many other athletic achievements we can strive towards. When we are really attached to something we want, so very badly, to accomplish, it becomes an act of profound bravery to let it go and move on.

Of course, this too needs to be balanced. The sub-dimensions of AQ are not bad or good in and of themselves. Grit, Mental Flexibility, both have upsides and downsides and we are all a unique combination of these ingredients that make up our Adaptability Quotient. In certain contexts, low Grit can be helpful (if it allows us to let go of a previous set goal, which is no longer relevant). In other contexts, low Grit might become a negative, especially if we have a tendency to abandon challenges too early.

However, as I mentioned earlier in this book, human beings have a tendency to over-emphasise and give excessive credence to the negative. I know very few people pursuing truly unattainable dreams and far more who gave up right before they might have achieved their wildest ambitions—sad though it is to say!

This is why rapid feedback loops—and the continual learning process—are so vital. They allow us to continually check in with ourselves, with our goals and objectives, and ask the question of whether they still serve us and our ambitions.

AQ is not a ranking system, where we value more highly adaptive people over less adaptive. It is a measure that provides self-insight and allows us to determine how we might improve ourselves and develop our adaptability muscles. Our mission at AQai is:

TO INSPIRE & EMPOWER EVERY HUMAN WITH THE SKILLS TO ADAPT AND THRIVE. ENSURING NO-ONE IS LEFT BEHIND IN THE FASTEST PERIOD OF CHANGE IN HISTORY.

This means helping people get to the next stage of their adaptability journey, wherever they might be.

But it also means not leaving *yourself* behind.

You owe it to yourself—to invest in your skills, to curate your teams, to become your best Self. And you owe it to everyone around you who will benefit from your becoming the best version of yourself. We are able to serve not only more people but more powerfully when we are able to rise up. By doing so, we start to have a positive impact on those around us, and the ripples of this can travel surprisingly far indeed.

We discussed the many different facets of Community—technological and human—and that Community is a multiplier of both positive and negative aspects of Self. Communities are unquestionably powerful. In fact, it is often *small* groups of people, tight-knit communities, that have changed the world, rather than large organisations or governments. One need only look to Christ and his Twelve Apostles as an example of this. Whatever your spiritual beliefs, one cannot deny they were pretty influential! As leaders, we must harness this tremendous power for good.

One phrase that has been repeated frequently on the news of late is Mass Hysteria. This is the psychological phenomenon where the fear response becomes so tangible it can pass—like a viral infection—from person to person so that eventually a person who has no relationship with the perceived threat still experiences the same level of terror. We know this phenomenon is real because we've seen it playing out all around us—especially in the midst of the Covid-19 pandemic and now with the looming uncertainty of expanding military conflict in the East. But what many people do not consider is this process can be reverse-engineered, for good. With the power of Communities, by becoming our best selves and setting an example, we can create Positive Hysteria. Your own positive acts and impact can reach far beyond those who are directly engaged. You can influence and have the same effect on others, not in direct contact with your acts. This has the potential to create a wave of positive behavioural shifts so large we can rewrite the very foundations of our society.

It's time to start the movement toward positive change.

EXERCISE 23:

CREATE A PLAN FOR HOW YOU WILL NOT LEAVE
YOURSELF BEHIND. 1ST - THINK ABOUT WHO DO YOU WANT
TO BECOME IN 12 MONTHS TIME?

....

....

....

....

....

....

....

....

2nd - When you consider who you want to become, 12 months from
now, looking backwards from there...

WHAT ARE THE 3 BIGGEST ACTIONS YOU COULD BEGIN TO
TAKE TODAY, WHICH WOULD SIGNIFICANTLY ENHANCE YOUR
CHANCES OF ACHIEVING YOUR VISION?

What might this look like?

What habbits/behaviours might you need to unlearn?

Spending more/less time with specific people?

More training?

Learning new skills?

Diversifying your portfolio?

Or taking a radically different approach?

1. ....

....

....

....

2. ....

....

....

....

3. ....

....

....

....

SUMMARY FOR PART 6

→ IF WE CAN EMBRACE THE ADAPTIVE CYCLE AND ENGAGE IN DAY-TO-DAY RAPID FEEDBACK LOOPS WE BECOME LIFELONG LEARNERS WHO CAN AVOID STAGNANT PITFALLS

→ "FAILURE" CAN SPRINGBOARD OUR GREATEST SUCCESSES

→ SHIFT FOCUS TO CREATING VALID AND ROBUST ADAPTATION AND INNOVATION METHODOLOGIES, OVER SPECIFIC "ANSWERS"

→ TECHNOLOGY IS ALSO PART OF OUR COMMUNITY; CONSIDER ITS IMPACT

→ GIVE YOURSELF PERMISSION TO LET GO OF YOUR GOALS IF THEY NO LONGER SERVE YOU

1 What is Moonshot Thinking - https://youtu.be/pEr4j8kgwOk
2 https://www.ncbi.nlm.nih.gov/pubmed/11466595
3 Harvard Business Review, "The Dark Side of Resilience", Tomas Chamorro-Premuzic, Derek Lusk, 2017.

PART 7: THE PARADOX OF LEARNING & UNLEARNING

KNOWLEDGE IS NO LONGER POWER

Most senior leaders may well feel they have gotten to where they are now because of their knowledge base. The "standard" pathway is to become an expert in something, manage others, and then eventually become so preeminent that one starts to "train the trainers". In some instances, it's expected that the knowledge we acquired in the first twenty-one years of our lives should for the most part see us through the next fifty, sixty, or beyond.

The value our society places on knowledge is encapsulated in the maxim "knowledge is power". Consider the way big brands guard their secrets, such as the eleven herbs and spices of Kentucky Fried Chicken or the ingredients of Classic Coke. The patent industry is built on the protection of ideas and knowledge. IBM still holds the top spot for most issued US patents at 8,540 in 2021, followed very closely by Samsung with 8,517. Both almost double the third position with LG corporation at 4,388. We feel an intermixture of awe and suspicion surrounding any organisation that guards or hoards knowledge (such as "secret" societies like the Freemasons). The concept of "gnosis" and "secret wisdom" is ingrained in the infrastructure and language of our civilisation. For example, if you "steal" my idea, I can take you to court and sue you. That knowledge belongs to me. It's my secret! Even in today's age of so-called "reason", we have a superstitious outlook on the value and power of "knowing" something. Those who "know" are gods we worship, hoping they will impart that knowledge to us (and we fully expect this imported knowledge will come at a price). Therefore, when we're told we need to "unlearn" something, it can shake us to our foundations and make us feel very vulnerable indeed.

Not only this, but on a biological level, we are ill-suited to unlearning. Hebb famously said that "Cells that fire together, wire together" and, more formally, "any two cells or systems of cells that are repeatedly active at the same time will tend to become 'associated,' so that activity in one facilitates activity in the other". This is based on the neurology of how our brains function. Learning is reinforced through the act of repetition on a cellular level. When you initially perform an action or explore an idea only two neurons fire together. But subsequent repetitions will cause *three* to fire together, forming a linked circuit. Going forward, whenever one of the neurons would fire in response to stimuli, *all three* fire because the neurons have been trained to react as one. This is the cause of Pavlov's conditioning: the dogs only salivated when they heard the bell, not when the food was placed before them because the neurons responsible for salivation were rewired to only activate and fire when the bell was rung!

But the conditioning doesn't stop there. With further repetition, the myelin sheath around the axon (see the diagram below of the neuron basics) is actually strengthened, meaning that our bodies and brains literally protect previously established knowledge in a casing! The benefits of this process are increased speed, accuracy, and autonomic function. This is why pianists can play at such seemingly impossible speeds because the circuits and myelin sheath have been so reinforced, the neurons so hardwired, the activity is thoughtless and automatic.

NEURAL LEARNING, GOOD FOR REPEATED USE, BAD FOR UNLEARNING

UNLEARNING IS HARD FOR THE BRAIN. THE MORE WE 'HARD-WIRE' THROUGH REPEATED PRACTICE & REWARD, THE MORE INSULATED, & INTERCONNECTED THAT THOUGHT, ACTION & BELIEF BECOMES.

INSPIRED BY: GROWTH MINDSET POCKET BOOK. BARRY HYMER & MIKE GERSHON

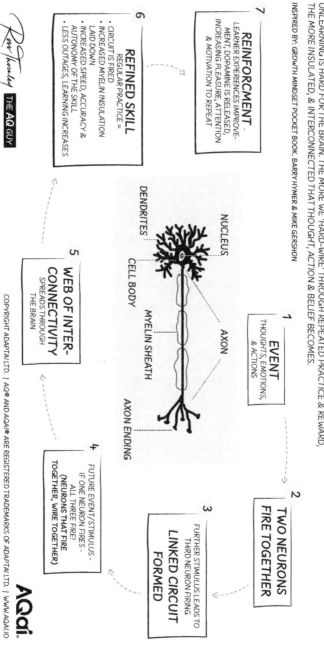

7 REINFORCEMENT -
LEARNER EXPERIENCES IMPROVE-MENT, DOPAMINE IS RELEASED, INCREASING PLEASURE, ATTENTION & MOTIVATION TO REPEAT

6 REFINED SKILL
REGULAR PRACTICE =
- CIRCUIT IS FIRED
- INCREASED MYELIN INSULATION LAID DOWN
- INCREASED SPEED, ACCURACY & AUTONOMY OF THE SKILL
- LESS OUTAGES, LEARNING INCREASES

5 WEB OF INTER-CONNECTIVITY
SPREADS THROUGH THE BRAIN

DENDRITES
NUCLEUS
CELL BODY
MYELIN SHEATH
AXON
AXON ENDING

1 EVENT
THOUGHTS, EMOTIONS, & ACTIONS

2 TWO NEURONS FIRE TOGETHER

3 FURTHER STIMULUS LEADS TO THIRD NEURON FIRING
LINKED CIRCUIT FORMED

4 FUTURE EVENT/STIMULUS -
IF ONE NEURON FIRES ALL THREE FIRE!
(NEURONS THAT FIRE TOGETHER, WIRE TOGETHER)

THE AQ GUY

AQai.

As you can imagine, going against this biological process—a core part of our makeup—is very difficult indeed. No wonder we react in horror when we're told we might need to let go of our old models!

In an exponential world, where virtually no process is safe from disruption, what we learned yesterday is likely not going to be as beneficial today. A good friend of mine is a millennial and he remembers his generation was emphatically told, growing up, that one couldn't make a living playing video games. A cursory search of YouTube reveals that this "knowledge" has been thoroughly disproved in today's world!

Knowledge may be fixed, but *learning* is constant.

EXERCISE 24:

CONSIDER YOUR ORGANISATION'S ATTITUDE TO "KNOWLEDGE".

Is information freely disseminated to employees or are there "tiers" and hierarchies that create barriers?

Is there valuable information that could be distributed in order to help employees at all levels?

....

....

....

....

....

RELEASING PAST CHOICES

In the past, key triggers would cause us to reevaluate where we were in life. These triggers might be getting fired from a job, turning a certain age, deciding to retire, or perhaps a change in our relationship status. These moments of soul-searching are idiomatically expressed in everyday phrases: "a mid-life crisis", turning "the big three-oh" or "sixty being the new forty". We have preconceived notions of benchmarks, either correlating to age, income or some other barometer, where we are almost expected to take a step back and ask ourselves whether we're on the right path.

Now, given the speed of change, we have to reevaluate on a much more consistent basis. This is challenging, especially when we have an emotional attachment to the knowledge or thinking that "got us here". Coleridge, one of the most talented romantic poets in the world, became addicted to opium partly because his personality was addictive but partly **because it became part of his creative process.** Having produced such wondrous (though incomplete) poems as *Kubla Khan* under the drug's influence, he believed he needed the drug in order to create, and ultimately he was unable to let go of this paradigm, leading him down a tragic path of self-destruction. This is obviously an extreme example, but the lesson is the same. We must reevaluate our processes, paradigms, strategies, and knowledge bases and ask ourselves whether they still serve us or are doing more harm than good.

In 1988, DNA was used in the UK for the first time to convict Colin Pitchfork, a suspect in two murders in Leicestershire. A year prior, in the United States, DNA testing was first used in the case of Tommy Andrews, a Florida rapist, who was accused of raping a woman during a burglary. Because of DNA testing, Tommy Lee Andrews was convicted because of the proven DNA that matched the DNA that was collected from the crime scene. Tommy Lee Andrews was sentenced to 22 years in prison after he was convicted of this crime.

Since then, crime scene DNA testing has come a long way, with many developments improving its accuracy and efficacy. However, even today, with all our immense advancements in the field, **DNA is still almost never used to exonerate previously convicted criminals.** This is largely because the legal system, and many judges, do not want to appear to have been wrong—nobody wants their knowledge, experience, and expertise to be seemingly undermined.

In the book *Black Box Thinking,* by Matthew Syed, he shares the story of Juan Rivera who was falsely convicted of rape and murder in 1992 and spent the following 13 years in prison. Even though DNA testing had been used 5 years earlier, it took until 2004 until police finally agreed to test the evidence from the case—and found he was innocent. Incapable of admitting their mistake (because it was a grave one), it took another 7 years until Rivera was finally released (and paid a $20 million settlement).

For the prosecutors, admitting their serious mistake would probably have meant they risked losing their jobs, and destroying their confidence—so they didn't.

Admitting mistakes is tough, but it's the only way to prevent making even worse ones. If you can start by admitting to yourself that you made one, you're one step ahead.

And still today there are 2,450 men and women on death row. To date, eighteen people have been proven innocent and exonerated by DNA testing in the United States after serving time on death row. They were convicted in 11 states and served a combined 229 years in prison—including 202 years on death row—for crimes they didn't commit[1]. We have the means of determining many more of their innocence or guilt now, but the legal system has little interest in finding out for sure because the whole machinery of Law in the West is founded on the principle of right decision-making and personal integrity (and knowledge) of the people—judges, jurors, and criminal barristers—in charge of those decisions. If you undermine a past decision you might corrode the integrity of the person who made the decision. If you corrode the integrity of the people in the machine you undermine the machine itself, at least according to their thinking!

But this isn't the case at all.

These people did the best they could with the knowledge available. Now, new knowledge—in fact, a whole new methodology—has become available. We simply need to let go of the old decisions and embrace the gift of greater clarity as a result of technological advancement. There have only been 375 DNA exonerees to date, wrongly convicted people who served a total of 5,284 years between them. What else is the failure to reevaluate and let go of past decisions stopping us from achieving?

As hard as it may be, all of us need to free ourselves from past decisions. Maybe we made a mistake. Maybe a decision we made cost money, time, energy, a relationship, and even personal health or well-being. But we are not our past decisions. When we're truly adaptable, we have the opportunity to

MAKE A NEW CHOICE EACH DAY.

EXERCISE 25:

WHAT NEW CHOICE WILL YOU MAKE TODAY?

This could be something as small as eating a different breakfast or as big as changing your whole approach to the working day.

....

....

....

....

....

....

WHO WILL YOUR CHOICE IMPACT OTHER THAN YOURSELF?

How will you align your new choice to your current values, and experience each day anew to help you rewire your thinking?

....

....

....

....

....

NEVER SPLIT THE DIFFERENCE

Chris Voss's seminal work *Never Split The Difference* reveals the secret truth of how every interaction is in fact a negotiation, a hostage situation, and he shares deep insight into how to successfully negotiate one's way through life and out of danger. However, we not only have to become good negotiators with other people—we have to become great negotiators with ourselves.

When negotiating we have to find out what the other person (or we) want. In other words, we have to discover their motivations, for our motivators are our wants and needs writ large. I've mentioned my good friend James Sale a few times throughout this book, and as one of the world's leading experts on motivation and the creator of the Motivational Map®—a tool I used extensively in my previous business—says that "It is important to stress again that all motivators are good and equal; there is no such thing as a 'bad' motivational profile. There is only context: some profiles are more relevant to specific roles or situations."[2] The desire/motivation for money, for example, is not bad in and of itself. It is the context of the individual or organisation that might make it so.

Motivation has been a subject of fascination for me for over a decade. What drives us? How can we improve our drive? How do we put more motivational fuel in the tank when it's running low? Maintaining motivation can be a gruelling process of negotiation with ourselves.

Motivation and adaptability work together in a very specific way. The power of motivation is that it works like an addiction; and addictions, as we well know, are very difficult to break—but they do have uses!

For example, you might be addicted to certain processes that have long been obsolete and that ideally, you would need to unlearn. You might also be addicted to the "come back" feeling, bouncing back from a hard situation. Another good friend of mine was once a fencer (sword-fighter) at the international level and was actively known as "The Come-Back King" (it seems quite a few athletes have this epithet—thinking of Tyson Fury, here). My friend told me a story about his time as a high-level competitor. He had just lost a hard-fought Direct Elimination match by just a few points. He was packing up his gear, the bitter taste of defeat in his mouth, and a fencing coach—not his own but someone else who had been watching his matches—came up to him

The coach said, "You're an adrenaline junkie." My friend was perplexed. He had never been sky-diving and didn't particularly like rollercoaster rides or other classic adrenaline-fuelled activities. In fact, when he wasn't fencing, his main activities were reading and writing books. But before my friend could object, the coach explained what he meant: "You have to go down five points before you get going. You like to be the underdog. That's the only reason you lost that fight. You let him get seven points ahead before you really started fighting. If you'd fought from the beginning, you'd be through to the next round."

My friend realised the coach was right. In all of his previous matches, he had allowed the opponent to get ahead before really kicking into gear. It wasn't a conscious decision or a tactical play. He was subconsciously self-sabotaging himself because he was addicted to that underdog syndrome, the adrenaline rush of "clutching" when everything was against him. His nickname "The Come-Back King" had become part of his identity unconsciously, and even a point of pride for him. This led my friend to a journey of discovery in which he had to rewrite those behaviours and make a new choice.

Alternatively, some people use their addictions to motivate their behaviours. This is a process of intense self-negotiation. In other words: *I will give myself a cookie if I complete this pile of work.* One might argue that long-term this is an unhealthy practice and could lead to negative brain training, but we all know that short-term it can achieve results. Indeed, many addicts use this idea to short-circuit the addictive cycle. Every time they want to use it, they instead eat a cookie or go for a run. They reward the behaviour of not succumbing to the addiction, thereby writing a new pathway in the brain (which is easier than deleting an old one, as we've discovered).

So, how deeply are we prepared to negotiate with ourselves, then? Are we prepared to let go of our addictions in exchange for success and freedom? When we think of it this way, Chris Voss is right: it really is a hostage situation!

There is a very real-world example of addiction put to good use to be found in the story of the incredible Joe Polish. Joe is a fellow Freezone Frontier in the same Strategic Coach group as myself, led by Dan Sullivan. Joe has owned a marketing company since 1994, which is now a multi-million-dollar business. He's sold millions of dollars worth of books and has been called "one of the most connected people on the planet." He runs Genius Network, arguably the highest-level group in the world for marketing. He was described by Tony Robbins as "a force of nature."

Joe is, however, somewhat of a controversial character in the business world: cheeky, unafraid to play devil's advocate, and full of 'wisdom bombs' that cut almost a little too close to the truth: "The secret of success, this is kinda funny. What is the secret? Pretend you've already achieved it then offer to sell the secret to others... which could sum up pretty much most of the personal development industry."

Joe has become one of the most sought-after marketing experts in the world, but at one point he was, in his own words: "a dead-end carpet cleaner, freebasing cocaine." He tells the story of being high at his own graduation, and, one particularly bad day, having alcohol, weed, LSD and cocaine all flowing through his system at once.

Joe has an addictive personality, in more ways than one. He is charismatic in a way that keeps people coming back for more, he hooks you with his energy and giving nature, along with his very deep care and love for others. But he is also clearly someone who, once they start something, can't stop. Fortunately, Joe has managed to transform his addictions from negative self-destructive ones to positive habits: healthy eating, a cross-fitness regime, and mindful practices. To view this in line with our understanding of motivation in AQ-Character, he is moving towards a burning ambition (playing to win), a goal, rather than away from fear. He has used addiction as a driver of behaviour rather than an inhibitor.

This is what I would define as adaptable motivation. He's taken an aspect of himself, his negative motivations, and shifted them towards something positive. To be truly adaptable, we need to learn to do the same. To channel our motivational energy into new habits, new thought processes, and new success regimes. It's okay to switch motivation. In fact, James Sale's research tells us our motivations are likely to change approximately every eighteen months during periods of stability. However, during periods of intense change, such as the one we're undoubtedly going through now as a collective species, they can change every six or even three months! No wonder getting to what we want is so difficult—it's changing all the time, and we have to be able to adapt to those changes.

One of the core ways in which up-and-coming business people might well consider a shift in their motivation is the pursuit of financial success. Joe famously said: "People that say money can't buy happiness. That's kind of a stupid comment because I buy happiness all the time." At his $25K mastermind group, Joe hands out a sheet that has "Write a Swimming Pool" across the top, and a quote from Paul McCartney: "Somebody said to me, 'But the Beatles were anti-materialistic.' That's a huge myth. John and I literally used to sit down and say, 'Now, let's write a swimming pool'." It's okay to want to be successful. But of course, the focus—or perhaps we should say the *motivation*—should be to become successful by helping others.

As Joe expressed so beautifully, "The opposite of addiction is connection."

EXERCISE 26:

WHAT MOTIVATES YOU?

WHAT DO YOU REALLY WANT?

WRITE THIS DOWN WITHOUT SHAME OR SELF-CRITICISM.

....

....

....

....

....

....

....

....

Is there a self-negotiation required to achieve this?

Is there a past decision, self-limiting identity or label would you need to let go of?

What new pathways and ideas could you list to help you move toward what you want, right now?

NEXT, WRITE DOWN A LIST OF WHO YOU WANT TO BE BETTER CONNECTED TO. AND NEXT TO EACH THINK OF ONE WAY YOU MIGHT BE ABLE TO CREATE VALUE IN THE WORLD FOR THEM.

You will be surprised how this act can help adapt your perspective of your past decisions, and embrace the joy of rebirth and recreation.

....

....

....

....

....

....

....

....

....

THE IMAGINATION ECONOMY

A behaviour most often becomes "acceptable" when it is repeated. AA fostered acceptability. Eventually, it becomes a "new norm". Consider how many aspects of lockdown have now become mainstays of everyday living.

However, often our concept of what is "acceptable" limits our thinking. Addiction, for example, is a taboo topic, yet certain "addictions" are considered acceptable. For example, how certain societies celebrate workaholism. In Japan, workaholism is so commonplace they have a specific word for suicide through over-work: *karoshi*. We condemn this in the West yet we are, in truth, extremely close to it ourselves. Similarly, addiction to fitness is considered okay, even when there is abundant evidence working out constantly actually puts a lot of strain on the body, and the healthiest people know when to rest and recover! This is because when we think in terms of what is acceptable and unacceptable we are thinking in a polarising way. In other words, we tend to view the world as being made up of conflicting opposites rather than as a continuum of a whole. For example, you're either straight or gay, white or black, left or right wing, happy or sad, successful or a failure, and on and on it goes. The celebrated author and host of the Magical Writing podcast S. C. Mendes says that "We view the world as a polarity. We either want to pull something towards us or we want to repel that thing away—it's like the poles of a magnet. Our biggest problem is changing that perception, but if you can, limitless possibilities open up to you."[3] Mendes goes on to make the point that if you look at the ancient Chinese symbol of the yin-yang, in each half, there is a spot of the other. So, in the black of yin, there is a single spot of white, and in the white of yang, there is a single spot of black. Neither is entirely one thing or the other!

We can apply this to ourselves and our business. Does being a mother mean we cannot be a successful business woman? Does having an organisation focused on making a positive impact on others mean we cannot generate revenue? Are these things really mutually exclusive or only because of societally entrenched beliefs?

Knowledge can also be limiting when we set too much store by it. The secret to successfully navigating and thriving in this period of intense change is to constantly reevaluate what we know, and that includes what we think we know about ourselves: our habits, addictions, motivations, environment, and ambitions—and adapt accordingly. Through this process, we shift from perpetuating a "knowledge economy" to creating an "imagination economy". In an era where a simple Google Search can answer 95% of our basic questions, knowledge is no longer the currency it once was. Instead, we need to be able to imagine brighter futures liberated from the decisions of the past and the negative addictive cycles that have held us back. In Part 1 of this book, we discussed the inherent negative cognitive bias we all have to deal with (I call this "tackling the biological system"). One other outcome of this bias is that we tend to use our imagination to picture everything that could possibly go wrong. In fact, many companies actively reward employees for anticipating obstacles or dangers—consultants are paid for this exact service to a degree. This harkens back to the prophets, soothsayers, and fortune tellers of ancient times being consulted as to whether the storm would pass over or continue, whether the crops would grow or whether disaster would strike. There is great value in identifying obstacles, but not at the cost of our confidence to imagine more boldly.

Moving towards an imagination economy, however, we have to shift the balance of our thinking from this age-old paradigm. We have to also reward those who can dream of brighter futures not portend doom. Yes, we still need to be able to deal with the obstacles when they come up (or to bounce forward with Resilience!)—this isn't a denial of reality—but we also have to be able to ask the question,

"WHAT IF IT ALL WENT RIGHT?"

WHAT MIGHT BE POSSIBLE THEN?

How often have you given yourself permission to imagine a future unencumbered by failure or disaster? I suspect for many of us it is not very often, or perhaps only in childhood! We have to once more unlock this ability to be able to dream without the limitations of polarised thinking, to fully embrace paradoxical thinking that allows for two seemingly contradictory things to be true simultaneously.

Only then can we experience perpetual future confidence.

SUMMARY FOR PART 7

→ IN AN EXPONENTIAL WORLD VIRTUALLY NO KNOWLEDGE BASE OR PROCESS IS SAFE FROM DISRUPTION

→ KNOWLEDGE MAY BE FIXED, BUT **LEARNING** IS CONSTANT

→ WE MUST FREE OURSELVES FROM PAST DECISIONS TO MOVE FORWARD

→ TO SUCCESSFULLY SELF-NEGOTIATE WE HAVE TO DISCOVER OUR DEEPER MOTIVATIONS, VALUES, AND WANTS

→ SHIFTING OUR THINKING FROM AN ECONOMY OF KNOWLEDGE TO AN ECONOMY OF IMAGINATION WILL HELP US NAVIGATE AN EXPONENTIAL WORLD

1 https://innocenceproject.org/the-innocent-and-the-death-penalty/
2 Sale, James; *Mapping Motivation*; Gower; 2016.
3 https://www.youtube.com/channel/UCColHQeiixfmzcZHn7bjblg

PART 8: A MOVEMENT FOR PERPETUAL FUTURE CONFIDENCE

REWIRING OUR RELATIONSHIP WITH CHANGE

What is perpetual future confidence?

I created this phrase to embody a mindset whereby we don't need a state of knowing or certainty in order to thrive. Our "comfort zone" has been extended to include the VUCA world, and we can attain "comfort" even in volatility, uncertainty, complexity, and ambiguity. **ATTAINING PERPETUAL FUTURE CONFIDENCE IS ONLY POSSIBLE WITH A COMBINATION OF PERSPECTIVE, MINDSET, AND PRINCIPLES.**

1. PERSPECTIVE OF FUTURE CONFIDENCE:

Rather than looking for certainty externally, we find that certainty *internally*. Instead of seeking out more and more data to mitigate our fear with knowledge, we recognise we have the skills and belief to take on whatever challenge the universe throws at us, and turn that challenge into an opportunity. This doesn't mean we "ignore the numbers" or the reality, of course, but it reflects a change in our response through the empowerment of peace and understanding.

2. MINDSET OF FUTURE CONFIDENCE:

So much research has been conducted on the power of mindsets that it is almost redundant to reiterate it here. Suffice it to say your mind has a disproportionate influence over not just everything you consider your "Self", but also the external world. Dan Sullivan's book *My Plan For Living to 156* is, I think, the perfect model and paradigm for changing our mindsets and belief because he is challenging one of the most deeply ingrained narratives of human existence: that we're going to die somewhere between the age of sixty and one hundred. Old fashioned phrases such as "three-score and ten" have ingrained the idea of a terminal point around this age. Frequent uproar at the increase in retirement age is testimony to the fact that people still believe they will be unable to work, or valuably contribute to society, beyond a certain age.

But is this a scientific fact? Or is this commonly held belief about to be significantly challenged by Dr David Sinclair and his work on epigenetics, together with new leaps in technology such as bio-printing, medicine, and our understanding of diet and biology?

Dan Sullivan is in his seventies. Yet, with his book *My Plan For Living to 156*, he visualises an extended lifespan: "I consciously wondered what would happen to my thinking if instead of seventy-five or eighty, I talked myself into thinking of my lifespan as 156 years. In doing so, I found that every time I thought about my lifespan, it made me feel young. I started to feel I had an enormous amount of time available to me, but I'd noticed the opposite happening to people in the business community who were in their forties and fifties: they felt that they were getting old and running out of time."

What are the benefits of feeling like we have more time ahead of us? Having a mindset of wanting to live to 156 has changed his outlook on health.

PARADOXICALLY, HE CARES MORE ABOUT HIS PRESENT-DAY DECISIONS BECAUSE HE'S THINKING LONG-TERM AND TRYING TO MAKE SURE HE DOES EVERYTHING POSSIBLE TO LIVE.

He makes better health choices, whether that be exercise, diet, or mindfulness. In his own words: "You get more focused on the real meaning and value of your present circumstances."

But the change is deeper even than that. By changing his mindset, Dan has created "extra years" or "bonus time" that he didn't believe he had previously. He can now make decisions about what to do with this extra time and when to "take it". He has conceptually created a resource for himself, specifically for self-development. Because the time is "extra", it feels like a gift, an addition, and so the possibilities of using it are endless.

To illustrate the inverse of this, Dan gives a powerful example where, during one of his seminars, he asked people to write the age at which they believed they were going to die. One member wrote down the answer forty-seven. How old were they? Forty-six!

When queried as to why they had given such a morbid answer, it turned out that no member of his family had lived past this age. In addition, subconsciously, he was already living as if this was his terminal point. He was drinking heavily, overweight, and regularly turned down opportunities to meet new people.

OUR BELIEFS CREATE OUR REALITY.

After working with Dan through a coaching program, this individual turned their life around. Dan says he saw him again at sixty, and for the first time, he was in a long-term relationship, a relationship that had started three years after the age at which he had previously been sure he would die. By transforming his mindset, he had immeasurably improved his life, deepened his relationships with others, and literally extended his lifespan. The power of mindset is quite overwhelming. Dan explains: "You don't have to work at this. The change in number is what brings on the changes in thinking because you immediately discover the thoughts and plans you had were based on your previous thinking about how long you were going to live." In other words, we don't even have to put much effort into the change. Really, by changing the number, we change the thought process, the actions following those thoughts, and consequently the reality around us.

Dan is a living embodiment of his principles. In his seventies, he is living his most successful, happy, and nourishing life to date. His business, Strategic Coach, is still expanding, and he is still leading it. Intriguingly he says: "The worst decade of my life was between the ages of thirty and forty..." which is what most people regard as their "prime".

The worst thing someone can do for their mindset, according to Dan, is to retire: "When people talk about retirement, they start talking themselves into an early grave. They stop learning new things, stop developing new things, stop building relationships, and stop meeting new people." I find this quote particularly profound because it correlates so effortlessly with our model of adaption.

Mindset has a key role to play in how we adapt to change. The best thing we can do is, rather than waiting for change to come, to precipitate it by altering our mindset now. The rest will follow.

3. PRINCIPLES OF FUTURE CONFIDENCE:

Our thoughts and ambitions are both hampered and multiplied by two primary inputs: our Environment and our Body. By "Body", I mean not just any physical difficulties we might have, such as a disability (though certainly, these can challenge us), but also the biological hardwiring within us we have to rewire and quieten. The foundational principle of developing our AQ mindset and perpetual future confidence is that our belief shapes our reality. Human beings have intuitively known this since the dawn of time, it seems. However, knowing is only half the battle—perhaps less than half! It is one thing to know your belief shapes your reality and your outcomes and quite another to put it into practice and live it!

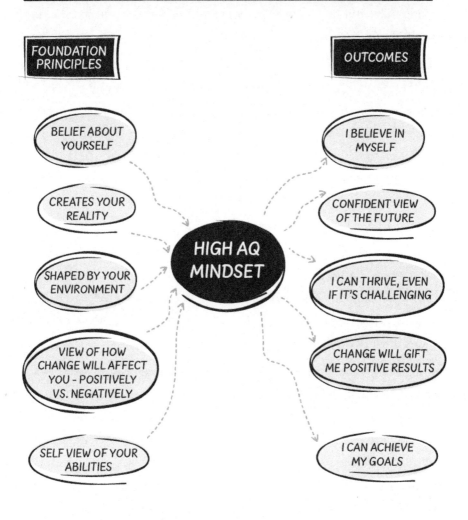

YOUR MINDSET FRAMES & INFLUENCES YOUR BEHAVIOUR, ACTIONS & OUTCOMES

FOUNDATION PRINCIPLES

OUTCOMES

BELIEF ABOUT YOURSELF

CREATES YOUR REALITY

SHAPED BY YOUR ENVIRONMENT

VIEW OF HOW CHANGE WILL AFFECT YOU - POSITIVELY VS. NEGATIVELY

SELF VIEW OF YOUR ABILITIES

HIGH AQ MINDSET

I BELIEVE IN MYSELF

CONFIDENT VIEW OF THE FUTURE

I CAN THRIVE, EVEN IF IT'S CHALLENGING

CHANGE WILL GIFT ME POSITIVE RESULTS

I CAN ACHIEVE MY GOALS

Ross Thornley THE **AQ** GUY

AQai.

Shifting our perspective, mindset, and principles is even more difficult when we consider the viral nature of social and societal behaviours. Covid-19 provides us with a number of examples of this in action, such as the frenzy of panic-buying toilet roll that momentarily left virtually every supermarket in the UK bereft of this basic utility.

At no point did any government or corporate authority ever give an indication there would be a shortage of toilet roll, yet at some point someone had the thought: *What if this lockdown goes on for a long time and there is an issue with toilet roll production?* Rather than responding to this thought by giving it due consideration, they reacted to the thought and decided to go out and panic buy—I don't condemn them, it's simply something that happened, almost like a biological imperative.

Once one person did it, others saw them and thought, *Wait a minute, they're buying all the toilet roll—what if I don't get my share?* This kind of thinking is rooted in the narrative of scarcity, that resources are few and far between and must be hoarded. Soon, more and more people are buying toilet rolls in bulk even though **there is no scarcity**. It is totally imagined! Once the media starts reporting on it, naturally things get even worse!

Going against the grain of these viral reactions is not easy. We are communal creatures. We long for acceptance and the safety of social constructs, even the introverts among us. In Maslow's Hierarchy, "belonging" is only one step away from pure physiological needs such as food, water, and shelter! As James Sale writes in *Mapping Motivation*, "The truth is that human beings do not start life as adults, but as little babies, and in that condition, they cannot 'achieve' security or very much else: they cannot feed, clean, or protect themselves. What they learn implicitly for the first two years of their life is that security – living itself – depends on another, the carer or parent who looks after and hopefully loves the infant."

In Harry Harlowe's seminal study conducted on infant rhesus monkeys[1], researchers constructed two fake "monkey mums". One of the monkey mothers was a wire and wood skeleton, harsh and cold to touch. The other monkey's mother was covered in foam rubber and soft terry cloth. Two tests were set up. In test 1, the wire skeleton was given the baby milk. In test 2, the cloth mother had the milk. The question the researchers wanted to know was: which mother would the baby rhesus monkeys choose?

To their surprise, in *both* tests, the babies spent the majority of time with the warm, comforting mother, even when she didn't have the baby milk bottle.

Seeking comfort in stressful situations is hard-wired. Looking for the embrace of our mothers, our partners, and others' arms when we are in unfamiliar settings is natural. **If we are to survive in the exponential world of today,** a world that is only going to become more complex, volatile, uncertain, and ambiguous, we need to curate an environment with the people around us, our teams, and colleagues who can give a collective sense of safety to each other, amidst the turmoil—**to say nothing of actually thriving in such a world!**

The good news is, as I mentioned at the end of Part 6, virality works two ways. Just as we can create mass hysteria by influencing others with an aura of fear, so too can we pass on the kindness, care, confidence, and optimism. We do this by first redirecting our internal energy flow from the negative to the positive using the techniques we have covered in Parts 1 to 7 of this book. We then role-model this in our immediate communities.

When we embrace a mindset of perpetual future confidence, we are of course still aware of the negatives whether they are global, political, or personal, but the difference is we are not controlled by them.

In other words, we're free.

EXERCISE 27:

WHY NOT SEE HOW THINKING DIFFERENTLY ABOUT YOUR LIFESPAN SHIFTS YOUR TODAY - INSPIRED FROM DAN'S PLAN FOR LIVING TO 156?

What would your number be? ....

....

....

DOES THIS CHANGE ANYTHING?

How has your vision altered as a result of this new perspective, and future confidence?

....

....

....

....

....

....

....

....

NEW TERRITORY DISCOVERED

One analogy I have found particularly helpful when dealing with the dizzying concept of perpetual future confidence is this: when you are playing a video game, usually you begin the game with no map of the territory. As you explore, the map expands. Each time you reach an "edge", new territory reveals itself. Often, the map can end up being vaster than you ever imagined at the start of the game!

In many respects, this is an accurate reflection of the journey of discovery we must all embark on in order to realise our dreams and ambitions and attain perpetual future confidence. Rather than fearing the "edge" of the map, we must drive towards it, because only at the edge will the next stage, the next level, the new territory to explore, be revealed. Indeed, if we linger in the starting area and never approach the edge we will live the rest of our lives never knowing what lies beyond it or what our future could hold.

This also requires us to be flexible with our goal-setting. This is because we have to set goals in the here and now without knowing what lies beyond that edge, beyond the current horizon. The territory is going to change, and so we have to be capable of letting go of a goal that was founded on limited information—remember the stories of the judges and the inmates on death row; we have to release ourselves from past decisions when new information comes to light.

I often talk about creating a goal hierarchy but writing it all in pencil. This way we can evolve our thinking; our smaller goals which serve the higher goal can be rewritten as we uncover better ways to achieve our ultimate goal. And perhaps even our highest goal might evolve as we discover new territories and lands. If we hold ourselves too tightly to who we were, and where we are, we can't level up.

EXERCISE 28:

To help you focus on what you hold most important,

CREATE A GOAL HIERARCHY, WITH YOUR ULTIMATE GOAL AT THE TOP, AND YOUR "MEANS" GOALS IN LAYERS BELOW.

But write your "means" goals in pencil so that, when the time comes to reevaluate them via a rapid feedback loop, you can rewrite, replace and improve them.

My ULTIMATE GOAL ....

....

....

....

....

Five speciffic MEANS goals which will help me achieve my ultimate goal

1. ....

....

....

....

....

---

2. ....
....
....
....
....

3. ....
....
....
....

4. ....
....
....
....

5. ....
....
....
....

THE SUNK COST FALLACY

When rewiring our response to change, and moving toward this perpetual future mindset, one of the primary obstacles or "enemies" we can face is the "Sunk Cost Fallacy". This is the tendency of human beings to continue down a given path because they feel they have invested too much to withdraw; needless to say this can be inimical to adaptability!

The Decision Lab frames the Sunk Cost Fallacy beautifully: "The Sunk Cost Fallacy describes our tendency to follow through on an endeavour if we have already invested time, effort, or money into it, **whether or not the current costs outweigh the benefits.**"[2] That last part is critical because it reflects the **illogical component of human decision-making.** Even when the costs outweigh the benefits we continue because we have an emotional attachment to the "endeavour" or investment. We spoke earlier about a form of cognitive bias called "embodied cognition" but the Sunk Cost Fallacy correlates to another form of cognitive bias called "commitment bias", which **"describes our unwillingness to make decisions that contradict things we have said or done in the past.** This is usually seen when the behaviour occurs publicly."[3] Naturally this creates a negative loop.

A community can multiply the effect of the Sunk Cost Fallacy because commitment bias is partly sociological—in other words, it is correlated to how we think people see us and wish to maintain that image, even if the image is ultimately destructive to our ambitions.

We might think about this on an individual or even organisational level, but I invite you to now consider this is affecting the whole human race. The whole of human progress up to this point has been achieved—or so we believe—through a series of methodologies, and therefore we have a commitment bias *as a species* to these methodologies. We are, collectively, experiencing the Sunk Cost Fallacy playing out on a global scale. We have invested so much in a certain type of learning, in certain types of knowledge, in certain skills and beliefs; to change all that after two hundred thousand years seems ludicrous, impossible, dangerous even. But we must. And the time is now.

Yuval Noah Harari observed that "This seems patently unjust, one could argue that as long as there is a single child dying from malnutrition, or a single adult killed in drug lord warfare, humankind should focus all its efforts on combating these worlds. Only once the last sword is beaten into a ploughshare should we turn our minds to the next big thing. **But history doesn't work like that.**"[4]

We think there will come a time when it is "safe" to make this transition, but the fact is, that safe and certain time is never going to arrive. Safety and certainty is internal, it is within us, we just have to claim it.

Shakespeare once said, "There is nothing either good or bad but thinking makes it so."[5] When we are liberated from the tyranny of *reaction* and the fear response, we can choose what we need relevant to our situational context. As we mentioned before, sometimes fear is the more useful driver! That is what harnessing our adaptability intelligence and developing perpetual future confidence allows us to achieve: choice.

From this perspective, we realise that all "inputs" or "stimuli" are the fuel of one kind or another. Massive monetary loss is fuel—it is the burning platform we need to get into a deliberate fear state and reevaluate our processes and models. But so is a golden opportunity on the horizon that fires up our ambition! We can shift between these two spheres of thinking without committing wholeheartedly forever to one or the other. We can use both "negative" and "positive" experiences to grow and develop. Every failure, therefore, becomes a springboard for new growth. Every victory becomes, likewise, not an excuse to sit back and relax, but an opportunity to inspire new outcomes. This is a fairly unstoppable state of being! There is a reason I refer to adaptability as a superpower.

FINAL EXERCISE:

WHAT DO YOU CONSIDER TO BE YOUR NUMBER ONE OBSTACLE TO THRIVING?

....

....

....

....

....

DO YOU SEE A RELATIONSHIP BETWEEN THIS OBSTACLE AND A SUNK COSTS FALLACY?

....

....

....

LESSONS FROM THE MONKEY KING

We began this book with the evolution of humans from monkeys, and so it seems fitting that it should end with a story about a monkey too.

In traditional Tang Shao Tao Shaolin Kung Fu, an art form that is nearly lost as many of the temples were raided and the knowledge destroyed during the Chinese Communist regime, every practitioner undertakes to learn the "animal forms". These animal forms are fascinating and incredibly beautiful to watch. To me they show how human beings can reintegrate with their environment, not merely learning from the natural world but *becoming* the natural world. When you see a real Tang Shao Tao practitioner performing crane-style, it is almost as if you are observing the beautiful, elegant bird sweeping over a lake. In the practitioner's mind, they are the bird, and there is no duality or separation; as H. G. Wells observed, they are "an animal perfectly in harmony with its environment..." and therefore "...a perfect mechanism."

Whilst a student will learn many forms to increase their breadth and stretch their abilities, it is understood that they will have a natural preference for one, and in time this preference will lead to mastery. Though all the animals are considered "equal" as variations that suit different body types and psychological preferences (the patience of the Mantis or the ferocity of the Tiger might suit different people, for example) there is one exception: the Monkey King. The Monkey King is considered the highest and greatest of all the animals, ascending to a level of mythic grandeur in the lore and history of China. Even though the techniques of the original forms were lost to all but a few, the cultural reverence for the Monkey King and the stories of his exploits have endured for millennia. Why? Because the Monkey King embodies a state of "play". In other words, whereas all the animals typify different responses to fear and danger—the Serpent remains cool and level-headed, the Eagle rises above, the Lion brings its strength to bear—only the Monkey King is able to *laugh, to play*, and to *have fun in the face of fear*! This is the ultimate power of a transcendent state, to actually face a threat not with fear but with a smile. To turn mortal peril into an opportunity for fun and creativity.

Understandably, the road is long and hard to becoming the Monkey King and harnessing the superpower of adaptability in the face of tumult and change, but if we can use our Grit to keep expanding our passions, we might just overcome our deepest biological inhibitors and achieve the joy of true mastery.

SUMMARY FOR PART 8

→ PERPETUAL FUTURE CONFIDENCE IS A MINDSET WHEREBY WE DON'T NEED EXTERNAL EVENTS, A STATE OF KNOWING OR CERTAINTY IN ORDER TO THRIVE

→ ATTAINING PERPETUAL FUTURE CONFIDENCE IS ONLY POSSIBLE WITH A COMBINATION OF PERSPECTIVE, MINDSET, AND PRINCIPLES

→ AS SOCIAL CREATURES, REWIRING OUR COLLECTIVE RESPONSE TO CHANGE IS EVEN HARDER, BUT WE CAN USE OUR SOCIAL NATURES FOR GOOD

→ THE SUNK COST FALLACY CAN BE ONE OF OUR BIGGEST ENEMIES AND CHANGE-BLOCKERS

→ PLAY IN THE FACE OF "DANGER" IS THE ULTIMATE EXPRESSION OF AQ MASTERY

1 https://www.psychologicalscience.org/publications/observer/obsonline/harlows-classic-studies-revealed-the-importance-of-maternal-contact.html
2 The Decision Lab, https://thedecisionlab.com/biases/the-sunk-cost-fallacy
3 The Decision Lab; https://thedecisionlab.com/biases/commitment-bias
4 Harai, Yuval Noah; *Homo Deus*; Harvill Secker: 2015.
5 Shakespeare, William; *Hamlet*; circa 1600.

EPILOGUE

This book is an attempt to cover vast ground, to unlock far-distant continents occupying the frontiers of the territory we as a species are exploring. When setting out on this journey to "Decode AQ", I was faced with a decision: whether to paint the tree in broad strokes or go into minute detail of a single branch. AQ is a huge topic, a huge territory, and we are only beginning to uncover its full scope. Part of my life's work is to see not just the tree painted in detail but the entire forest. This cannot be achieved in isolation, nor do I want to "hoard" the concept of adaptability intelligence—adaptability belongs to humanity and I hope others will contribute their experience, ideas, and wisdom to the effort of unveiling the forest in all its majesty. Who knows, maybe, one day, we will be able to provide a map of this forest for future generations so that they might move forward in perpetual future confidence.

Ross Thornley

15.03.2022

APPENDIX

This appendix consists of data analytics drawn from 3,569 assessments collated in April 2022. The two main aims of conducting this analysis were (1) to understand "dimension correlation" across the fifteen sub-dimensions of AQ, and (2) to understand how demographic factors may or may not influence AQ scores.

In statistics, a correlation coefficient is a quantitative assessment that measures both the direction and the strength of this tendency to vary together. A correlation between variables indicates that as one variable changes in value, the other variable tends to change in a specific direction. Understanding this relationship is useful because we can use the value of one variable to predict the value of the other variable.

Correlation and causation are terms which are generally misunderstood and often used interchangeably.

Correlation refers to a statistical technique which tells us how strongly the pair of variables are linearly related and change together. It does not tell us the why and how of the relationship, merely that the relationship exists.

Causation goes a stage further than correlation. It says any change in the value of one variable will cause a change in the value of another variable, which means one variable makes the other happen. It is also referred to as cause and effect.

A good example to illustrate this is that ice cream sales are correlated to homicides in New York. When homicide numbers go up, so go ice cream sales. However, the relationship is not causal. The sale of ice creams does not increase the number of murders. There are likely multiple hidden factors that link these two. Such as the weather: when it's sunny, the ice cream vans operate and sell more. As more people are outside, potenitally murderers might have a greater opportunity to find vulnerable people. Perhaps the heat might also cause emotional triggers and agrivation too. Therefore the summer weather would be just one of multiple potential causal factors in this relationship.

Our findings reveal a number of correlations, in some instances, these correlations are might suggest a possible causal relationship, but much more data and investigation are needed to demonstrate this to the degree of scientific validity. In addition, though preliminary, our data set has also revealed some intriguing trends according to demographic factors. We share this data in an open way to encourage more questions, research and interest in the subject. We look forward to wider analysis and continued research over many years to come.

DEMOGRAPHIC DATA FOR THE AQME ASSESSMENT CHARTS SHARED:

Number of AQme Assessments **3,569** *(from April 2022)*

Gender

Female	49.9%
Male	45.8%
Prefer not to say	3.9%
Transgender	0.3%
Non Binary	0.1%

Region

Americas	57.62%
Europe	29.40%
Oceania	5.01%

Asia	4.33%
Africa	3.64%

Age

18-24	4.0%
25-39	38.7%
40-54	40.6%
55+	16.7%

AQ ABILITY CORRELATIONS

	GR	MF	MI	RE	UN
GR - GRIT	-				
MF - MENTAL FLEXIBILITY	0.48	-			
MI - MINDSET	0.47	0.36	-		
RE - RESILIENCE	0.33	0.32	0.44	-	
UN - UNLEARN	0.21	0.52	0.29	0.46	-

Note. N = 3,569. Guidelines for evaluating r are .10 = small, .30 = medium, .50 = large

AQ CHARACTER CORRELATIONS

	ER	EX	HO	MS	TS
ER - EMOTIONAL RANGE	-				
EX - EXTRAVERSION	0.35	-			
HO - HOPE	0.39	0.26	-		
MS - MOTIVATION STYLE	0.23	0.21	0.28	-	
TS - THINKING STYLE	0.28	0.27	0.32	0.3	-

Note. N = 3,569. Guidelines for evaluating r are .10 = small, .30 = medium, .50 = large

AQ ENVIRONMENT CORRELATIONS

	COS	EH	TES	WE	WS
COS - COMPANY SUPPORT	-				
EH - EMOTIONAL HEALTH	0.43	-			
TES - TEAM SUPPORT	0.66	0.42	-		
WE WORK ENVIRONMENT	0.6	0.48	0.72	-	
WS WORK STRESS	-0.17	-0.35	-0.13	-0.15	-

Note. $N = 3,569$. Guidelines for evaluating r are .10 = small, .30 = medium, .50 = large

15 AQ SUB DIMENSIONS CORRELATIONS

	GR	MF	MI	RE	UN	ER	EX	HO	MS	TS	COS	EH	TES	WE	WS
GR - GRIT	-														
MF - MENTAL FLEXIBILITY	0.48	-													
MI - MINDSET	0.47	0.36	-												
RE - RESILIENCE	0.33	0.32	0.44	-											
UN - UNLEARN	0.21	0.52	0.29	0.46	-										
ER - EMOTIONAL RANGE	0.42	0.41	0.52	0.54	0.36	-									
EX - EXTRAVERSION	0.28	0.29	0.4	0.27	0.28	0.35	-								
HO - HOPE	0.44	0.42	0.45	0.48	0.36	0.39	0.26	-							
MS - MOTIVATION STYLE	0.028	0.31	0.22	0.22	0.35	0.23	0.21	0.28	-						
TS - THINKING STYLE	0.37	0.45	0.35	0.19	0.23	0.28	0.27	0.32	0.3	-					
COS - COMPANY SUPPORT	0.31	0.27	0.36	0.21	0.19	0.26	0.24	0.29	0.12	0.25	-				
EH - EMOTIONAL HEALTH	0.41	0.33	0.5	0.43	0.24	0.57	0.25	0.44	0.11	0.26	0.43	-			
TES - TEAM SUPPORT	0.34	0.26	0.4	0.26	0.27	0.29	0.27	0.23	0.086	0.24	0.66	0.42	-		
WE WORK ENVIRONMENT	0.41	0.4	0.44	0.26	0.27	0.34	0.3	0.32	0.14	0.31	0.6	0.48	0.72	-	
WS WORK STRESS	-0.0012	-0.01	-0.11	-0.15	-0.06	-0.11	-0.0059	-0.086	0.0057	-0.0053	-0.17	-0.35	-0.13	-0.015	-

Note. N = 3,569. Guidelines for evaluating r are .10 = small, .30 = medium, .50 = large

HISTOGRAMS FROM AQME ASSESSMENT

Shown across each of the sub-dimensions

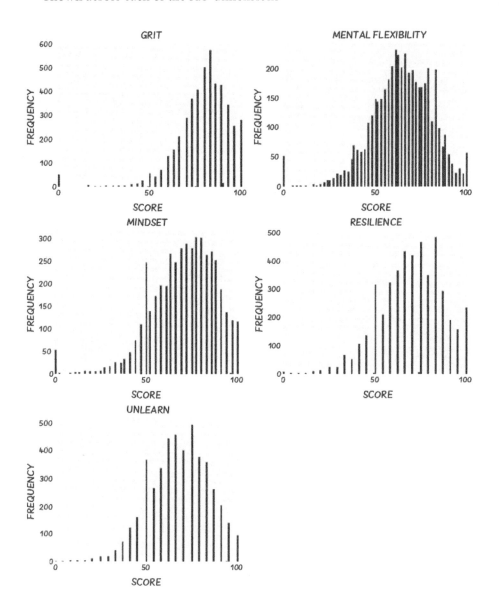

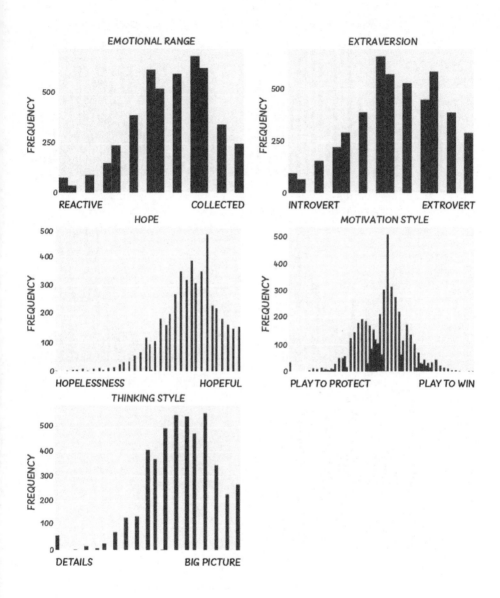

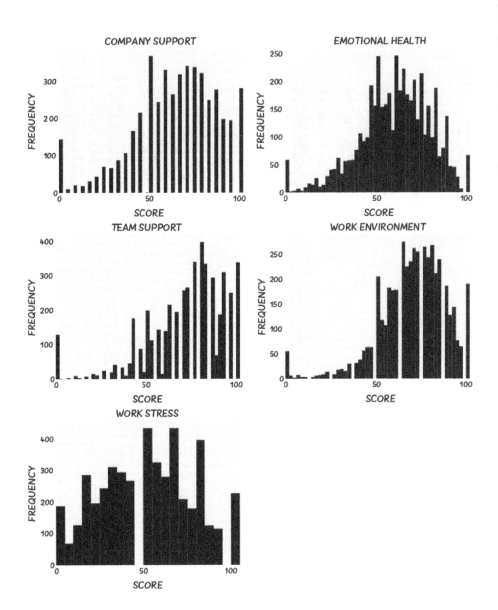

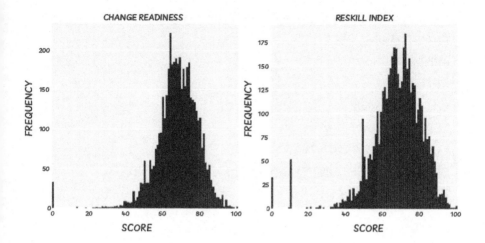

With so much information and ground to cover, I chose not outline several of our more advanced matrix and indexes in full detail, that is in this first version of the book! From our proprietary **Change Readiness** and **Reskill indexes**, to multiple adaptive behaviour indications found within our team reports. As a headline into the makeup of these, we have shared some information below. This does not go into the weighting or specifics of the algorithms used. However, by understanding the sub-dimensions involved you can begin to identify areas in which you can improve, and thus positively affect the index readings.

AQ CHANGE READINESS INDEX

We created our AQ Change Readiness Index, which indicates how easily you can adapt to challenges and organisational change. If an organisation is undergoing significant overhauls, whether structural, systemic, or strategic, it is important that employees are on board with these changes and properly equipped to handle them. The Change Readiness Index is reflective of the overall ability to cope with coming change. Please note: we are continually researching and collecting data to optimize our indexes with the goal of predicting how effectively employees will adapt.

Sub-dimension make up and impact, weightings vary (+ Positive, - Negative)

→ PLAY TO WIN   +
→ MINDSET   +
→ GRIT   +
→ EXTRAVERSION   +
→ TEAM SUPPORT   +
→ COMPANY SUPPORT   +
→ CHANGE UNCERTAINTY   -   (SPECIFIC QUESTION DATA)
→ EMOTIONAL HEALTH   +

Sub-dimension inclusion correct as Summer 2021. Subject to change through AQai® research and data.

AQ RESKILL INDEX

We created our AQ Re-Skill Index indicates how able you are to learn new skills, processes, or adopt new technologies. The higher the AQ Re-skill Index, the more likely employees will be able to learn new skills and the faster they will learn them. Our early insights show that employees who proactively move beyond their comfort zone, use diverse perspectives when searching for solutions, and overall are more confident, will master new skills quicker.

Sub-dimension make up and impact, weightings vary (+ Positive, - Negative)

→ UNLEARN   +
→ MENTAL FLEXIBILITY +
→ PLAY TO PROTECT   +
→ HOPE   +
→ WORKSTRESS   -
→ GRIT   +

Sub-dimension inclusion correct as Summer 2021. Subject to change through AQai® research and data.

Please find below several box plots charts to help visualise multiple distributions of variables. To help you understand the basics of box plots:

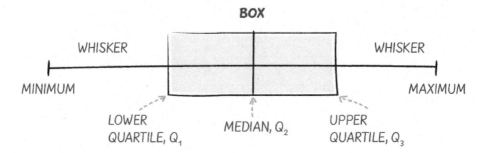

The left and right sides of the box are the lower and upper quartiles. The box covers the interquartile interval, where 50% of the data is found.

The vertical line that split the box in two is the median.

The whiskers are the two lines outside the box, that go from the minimum to the lower quartile (the start of the box) and then from the upper quartile (the end of the box) to the maximum.

AQ SCORE DISTRIBUTION BY WORK TENURE

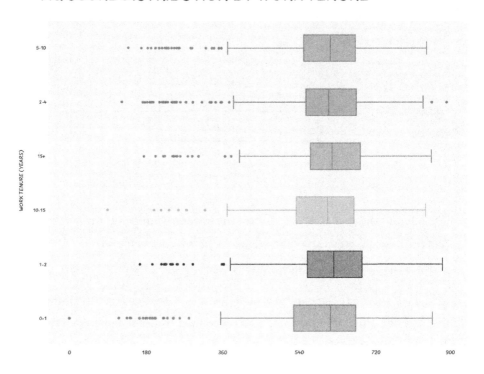

Work Tenure (Years)

Work Tenure (Years)	
0-1	19.45%
1-2	11.12%
2-4	21.32%
5-10	22.29%
10-15	10.51%
15+	15.31%

There is very little difference when looking at the work tenure across our this vast dataset.

However, this has proven to be highly valuable on a company by company basis. With the ability to drill down and filter data reports directly within the platform, clients have been able to isolate multiple points of opportunities to improve and strengthen adaptability within sub groups of their workforces.

AQ SCORE DISTRIBUTION BY JOB LEVEL

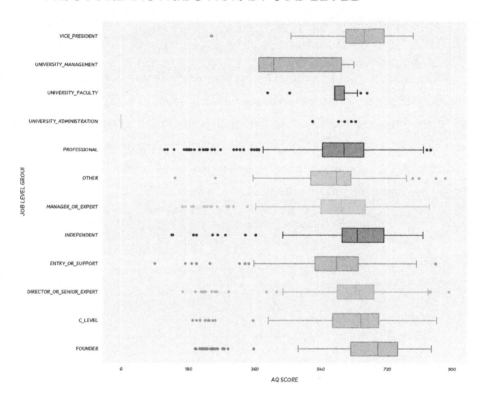

Job Level

Professional	25.16%
Manager or Expert	22.87%
Director or Senior Expert	15.54%
Entry or Support	8.29%

Founder	7.02%
C Level	5.76%
Independent	5.44%
Other	3.42%
Vice President	2.99%
University Administration	2.66%
University Faculty	0.54%
University management	0.31%

When we take a look at the AQ scores across different job levels, from this specific dataset, we can see fascinating patterns emerge. From the high adaptability of founders, and VPs. And the significantly lower scores for university management, entry level roles, and managers. An increase in AQ score correlates with the increase in job level. Indicating adaptability is a key aspect of career development and advancement.

AQ SCORE DISTRIBUTION BY GENDER

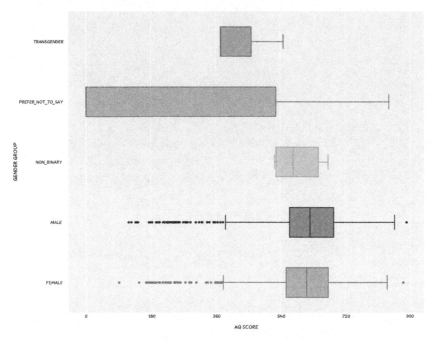

Gender

Female	49.9%
Male	45.8%
Prefer not to say	3.9%
Transgender	0.3%
Non Binary	0.1%

When we take a look at AQ scores across gender, of this specific dataset, we can see very little difference between male and female AQ scores. We have included the current outputs for non binary, transgender and those who would prefer not to say. However, the demographic data count for these are too low to accurately draw any insights at this stage. As we collect wider and larger data sets, it will be a good area to apply deeper research and analysis.

AQ SCORE DISTRIBUTION BY JOB FUNCTION

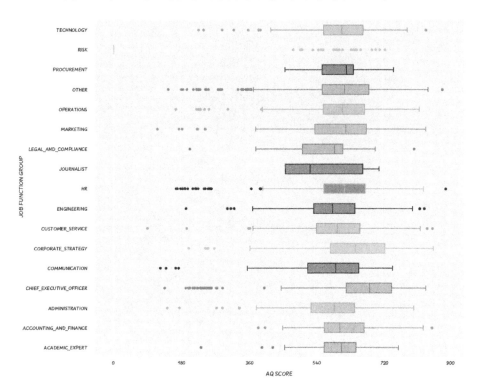

Job function

HR	18.35%
Other	17.15%
Engineering	10.14%
Chief Executive Officer	9.08%
Operations	8.25%
Technology	7.46%
Accounting & Finance	5.73%
Administration	4.75%
Marketing	3.65%
Risk	3.35%

Customer Service	3.33%
Corporate Strategy	2.90%
Communication	1.99%
Academic Expert	1.89%
Legal & Compliance	0.87%
Procurement	0.87%
Journalist	0.23%

Additionally, when we take a look at the AQ scores across different job functions, from this specific dataset, we can begin to observe potential challenge areas. Together with opportunities for peer adaptability skills sharing. With journalists scoring lowest on their adaptability, and CEOs the highest.

INDEX

ABOUT THE AUTHOR

Ross Thornley is an exponential leader, futurist, and adaptability pioneer. Living in the UK with his wife Karen, their two dogs, bee hive and rescue chickens, he balances the rapid technological world with a peaceful life in the New Forest, where they grow dozens of fruit and vegetables for their simple vegan lifestyle.

"Coach, Mentor, Entrepreneur and 'AQ' Pioneer. Author of Moonshot Innovation & AQ Decoded. Ross's work is opening up new frontiers in workplace education. Leveraging conversational AI and predictive analytics his company's platform enables people, teams and organizations to successfully navigate accelerating change. His ability to contextualize diverse and complex subjects, inspire and engage audiences makes him a highly sought after international speaker." **WALL STREET JOURNAL.**

At AQai, he is co-founder, CEO and master trainer, in flow when building the army of highly engaged and committed pioneers. Training over 170 coaches in the science and power of human adaptability in the first year of the program.

A passionate and prolific creator and educator. Amassing over 10,000 hours of workshop design, facilitation and keynotes over two decades. A serial-entrepreneur launching and growing multiple businesses across; innovation, branding, training and technology.

AQai (2018) transforming the way people and organisations adapt to change. Launching the first AQ (Adaptability Quotient) assessment and personalised digital coaching platform leveraging AI.

An eternal optimist, champion of abundance, and international speaker, he is the founder of 6 companies, including *RT Brand Communications* (2000, exit 2017), a globally trusted strategic branding agency that has worked with UN Volunteers, Thomson Reuters, Sony and numerous other blue chip clients; *Mug For Life®* (2009) a UK designed and manufactured reusable coffee cup, helping companies like HSBC, Amex, NHS, Science Museum and dozens of universities to achieve more sustainable waste policies by reduce single use disposable coffee cups and planting trees through their UK program; *Leaps® Innovation* (2017), a rapid, proven approach to moonshot innovation, idea generation and business challenges that empowers organisations to validate effective strategies, campaigns, new proposition development and solutions within days.

He's been a Strategic Coach® FreeZone Frontiers™ and 10X Member, Abundance A360 Member, and Singularity University Executive Program Graduate. Always excited by ambition, collaboration, and new models of thinking. Looking to connect ambitious people and solutions with communities, through creativity, intelligence and innovation.

His MTP is

TO UNITE, INSPIRE AND ACCELERATE THE BEST OF ALL HUMANITY.

www.AQai.io
https://www.linkedin.com/in/rossthornley/

Printed in Great Britain
by Amazon

21568159R00180